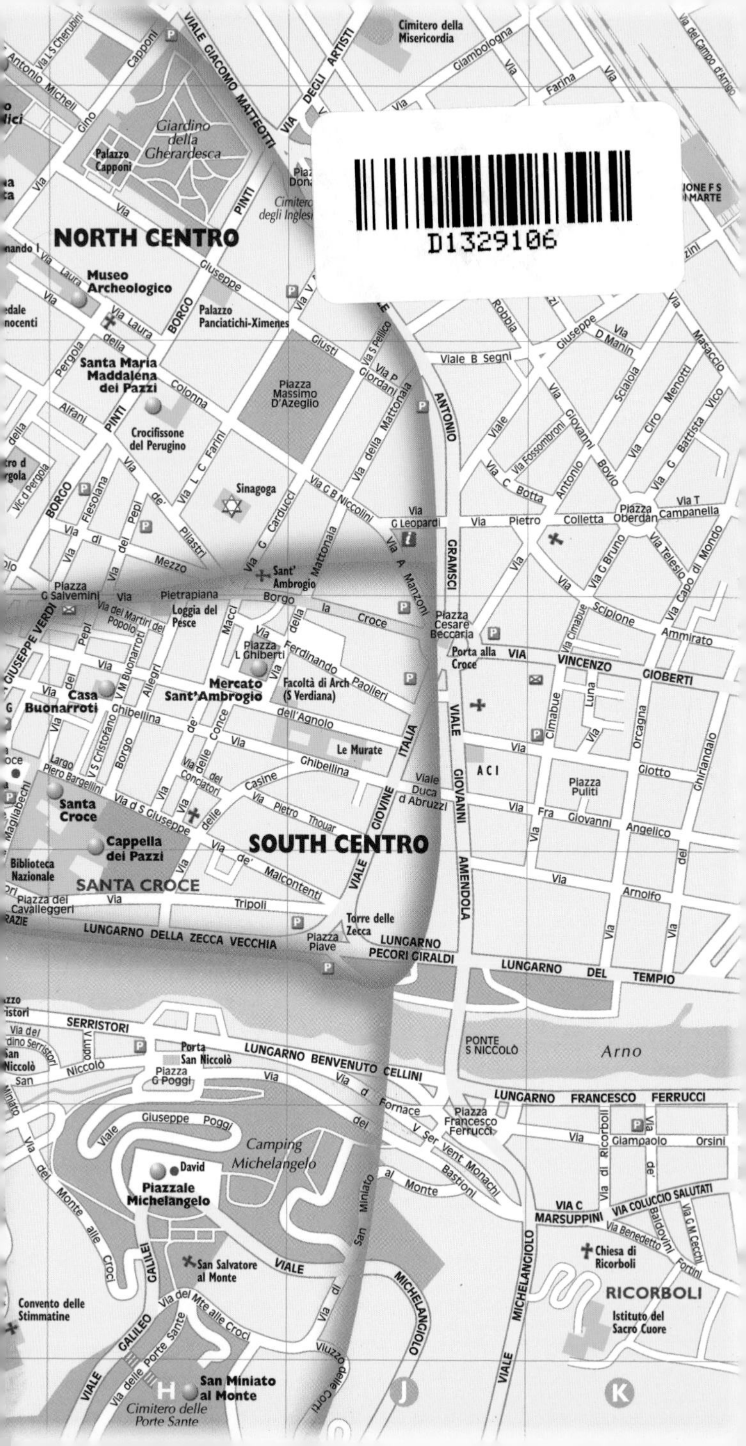

NORTH CENTRO
SOUTH CENTRO
SANTA CROCE
RICORBOLI
Cimitero della Misericordia
Giardino della Gherardesca
Palazzo Capponi
Cimitero degli Inglesi
Museo Archeologico
Palazzo Panciatichi-Ximenes
Santa Maria Maddalena dei Pazzi
Piazza Massimo D'Azeglio
Crocifissone del Perugino
Sinagoga
Sant' Ambrogio
Piazza G Salvemini
Loggia del Pesce
Piazza L Ghiberti
Mercato Sant'Ambrogio
Facoltà di Arch (S Verdiana)
Casa Buonarroti
Le Murate
Piazza Cesare Beccaria
Porta alla Croce
Piazza Oberdan
Piazza Puliti
ACI
Santa Croce
Cappella dei Pazzi
Biblioteca Nazionale
Piazza dei Cavalleggeri
Torre delle Zecca
Piazza Piave
LUNGARNO DELLA ZECCA VECCHIA
LUNGARNO PECORI GIRALDI
LUNGARNO DEL TEMPIO
Arno
PONTE S NICCOLÒ
SERRISTORI
Porta San Niccolò
Piazza G Poggi
LUNGARNO BENVENUTO CELLINI
LUNGARNO FRANCESCO FERRUCCI
Piazza Francesco Ferrucci
Camping Michelangelo
David
Piazzale Michelangelo
San Salvatore al Monte
Convento delle Stimmatine
San Miniato al Monte
Cimitero delle Porte Sante
Chiesa di Ricorboli
Istituto del Sacro Cuore
VIALE GIACOMO MATTEOTTI
VIA DEGLI ARTISTI
VIALE ANTONIO GRAMSCI
VIALE GIOVANNI AMENDOLA
VIALE GIOVINE ITALIA
VIA VINCENZO GIOBERTI
VIALE MICHELANGIOLO
VIALE GALILEO
VIA COLUCCIO SALUTATI
VIA C MARSUPPINI
H
J
K
D1329106

CITYPACK GUIDE TO
Florence

How to Use This Book

KEY TO SYMBOLS

- Map reference to the accompanying fold-out map
- Address
- Telephone number
- Opening/closing times
- Restaurant or café
- Nearest rail station
- Nearest bus route
- Nearest riverboat or ferry stop
- Facilities for visitors with disabilities
- Other practical information
- Further information
- Tourist information
- Admission charges: Expensive (over €8), Moderate (€5–€8), and Inexpensive (under €5)

This guide is divided into four sections

- Essential Florence: An introduction to the city and tips on making the most of your stay.
- Florence by Area: We've broken the city into four areas, and recommended the best sights, shops, entertainment venues, nightlife and places to eat in each one. Suggested walks help you to explore on foot.
- Where to Stay: The best hotels, whether you're looking for luxury, budget or something in between.
- Need to Know: The info you need to make your trip run smoothly, including getting about by public transport, weather tips, emergency phone numbers and useful websites.

Navigation In the Florence by Area chapter, we've given each area its own colour, which is also used on the locator maps throughout the book and the map on the inside front cover.

Maps The fold-out map accompanying this book is a comprehensive street plan of Florence. The grid on this fold-out map is the same as the grid on the locator maps within the book. We've given grid references within the book for each sight and listing.

Contents

Introducing Florence

Florence is one of the world's greatest art destinations, its famous museums and galleries, churches, palazzi and piazzas all crowded into a ravishing, compact *centro storico*. There's more to this historic gem than its art treasures, however: fashionistas, foodies and fans of the good life will not leave disappointed.

Shoppers here will find everything from chic designer shops and bespoke shoemakers to market stalls touting bargain leather goods and cheap jewellery. Florence's artisan tradition goes back centuries, and despite the pressures of the modern economy, you can still find furniture restorers and picture framers plying their trade in tiny workshops in the Oltrarno area of the city.

The thriving food and drink culture embraces everything from hole-in-the-wall wine bars and tripe stands to family-run trattorias and white-cloth gourmet establishments, while new cocktail bars are opening all the time.

Florence is more visitor-friendly than ever and large areas of the *centro storico* are now traffic-free. Museums have been revamped, there is a modern opera house and work on the much-awaited (albeit controversial) tram system is nearing completion. A younger, more energetic vibe is challenging the city's once-staid image of a living museum.

This is a city where blockbuster sights attract millions each year, so try to visit out of season (in the winter). If you can't avoid the crowds, seek out the lesser sights, many of which are hugely rewarding, and leave plenty of time for aimless wandering through cobbled backstreets and quiet piazzas. When it all gets too much, head out to the hills of Chianti for a breath of fresh air: this iconic, rolling landscape of vineyards, olive groves and cypress trees is right on the doorstep.

FACTS AND FIGURES

- Florence attracts around 6 million visitors a year.
- The native population is around 370,000.
- Florence has one of the lowest birth rates in Italy.
- The Uffizi Gallery is Italy's most visited museum—some 1.6 million visitors a year.
- In Italian the city is Firenze, but the original Roman settlement was called Florentia.

MATTEO RENZI

Florence-born Matteo Renzi, who became Italy's youngest prime minister in 2014, first emerged into the political limelight as mayor of Florence. His main legacy was the initiation of a general clean-up, which is still ongoing. Buildings were scrubbed, potholed roads mended and traffic banned from swathes of the city centre, creating a much pleasanter environment for everyone.

ON THE BALL

The Medici family, virtual sovereigns from the 14th to 18th centuries, left their mark on every building connected with them, so look out for their coat of arms, a varying number of balls *(palle)* on a shield, on buildings everywhere. The *palle* probably represent pills or coins, references to the family's original trade as apothecaries and later their role as bankers.

FLOOD FACTS

In November 1966 the River Arno burst its banks to disastrous effect: the tide, bludgeoning through the streets, reached as high as 6m (20ft) in the Santa Croce neighbourhood. This was not the only flood there has ever been, however: bridges were swept away in 1269 and 1333, and the city was submerged in 1557 and 1884, but not as badly as in 1966.

A Short Stay in Florence

DAY 1

Morning After breakfast head to the **Duomo** (▷ 58–59) and prepare to be awed by its mighty proportions; alongside are the superb **Campanile** (▷ 56) and **Battistero** (▷ 55). You can find out more about the history at the nearby **Museo dell'Opera del Duomo** (▷ 62). If you are feeling fit and don't suffer from vertigo, climb to the top of either the Duomo or Campanile for great views of the city.

Mid-morning Order a coffee at one of the café-terraces that line the traffic-free Piazza del Duomo to recharge your batteries. Head northwest up to **Mercato San Lorenzo** (▷ 68), the street market that now sprawls around the **Mercato Centrale** building (▷ 68). Traders here sell everything from knitwear to jewellery. It's known for its bargain leather goods—keep a look out for pickpockets and don't be afraid to haggle.

Lunch Opposite the northern flank of San Lorenzo church is the unassuming **Sergio Gozzi** (▷ 76), renowned for its Florentine cooking.

Afternoon Finish your shopping and then walk down Via dei Pucci and right into Via Ricasoli to the **Galleria dell'Accademia** (▷ 60–61) to view Michelangelo's massive masterpiece *David*. There's plenty more to see in the gallery, or you might prefer to backtrack and take in the Chapel of the Magi in **Palazzo Medici-Riccardi** (▷ 63).

Dinner For a special treat try **Hostaria Bibendum** (▷ 49) in the **Helvetia & Bristol** hotel in Via dei Pescioni (▷ 112). A cheaper option is **Belle Donne** (▷ 46–47), located close to **Via de' Tornabuoni** (▷ 36).

Evening Stroll down to the grandiose **Piazza della Repubblica** (▷ 39), with its triumphal arch, for a touch of Florentine atmosphere.

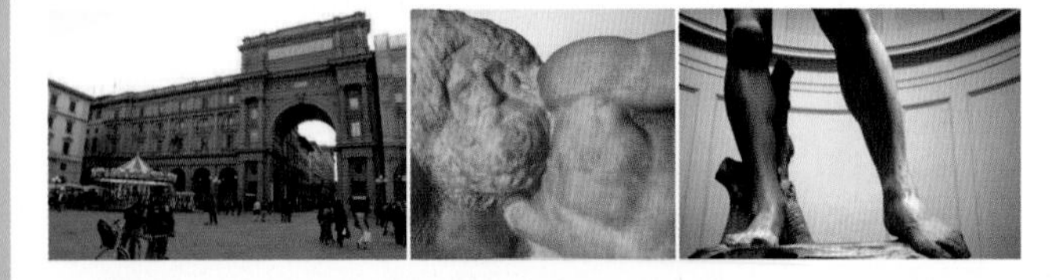

DAY 2

Morning Lines form from as early as 7am at the **Galleria degli Uffizi** (▷ 28–29), with its priceless paintings and sculptures, so get there as early as you can (or reserve ahead); be patient and you will be rewarded.

Lunch After you've seen all you want at the Uffizi, splash out and relax with a coffee on the terrace of historic **Rivoire** (▷ 50), the most elegant café on **Piazza della Signoria** (▷ 32). Alternatively, if you fancy something more substantial, tuck into hearty Tuscan cuisine at **Dei Frescobaldi** (▷ 48) on the opposite side of the square. Leave the piazza by its southwest corner, heading down Via Por Santa Maria, and stroll over the **Ponte Vecchio** (▷ 34–35) to be dazzled by its jewellery shops. There are plenty more gift shops just over the bridge.

Afternoon Take in the **Palazzo Pitti** (▷ 84–85). There are seven museums, plus the Royal Apartments to see, or if the weather is hot you might choose to stroll in the **Giardino di Boboli** (▷ 82). Palazzo Pitti is very popular, so be prepared to wait or book in advance. Then wander along to the church of Santa Maria del Carmine with the **Cappella Brancacci** (▷ 81) and its wonderful frescoes. The area is full of artisan workshops, boutiques and cafés and bars. If you are feeling fit, cross over Ponte Santa Trìnita and walk along the riverfront to **Santa Croce** (▷ 33).

Dinner The **Boccadama** (▷ 47) wine bar-cum-restaurant is in a nice spot to appreciate the lively square of Santa Croce.

Evening If the weather is kind you can get a great view of the city after dark from **Piazzale Michelangelo** (▷ 87) in the southeast of Oltrarno. Catch bus 13 to get there. Alternatively, take bus 7 up to the hill town of **Fiesole** (▷ 97) for wonderful views of Florence illuminated at night.

Top 25

TOP 25

Bargello ▷ 24–25 An overview of Florentine sculpture through works by Michelangelo and others.

Battistero ▷ 55 One of Florence's oldest buildings, famous for its mosaics and three sets of bronze doors.

Campanile ▷ 56 An incredible sight towering 85m (279ft) over the city, and offering great views.

Via de' Tornabuoni ▷ 36 The cream of world fashion is elegantly displayed on this street in the heart of medieval Florence.

Santissima Annunziata ▷ 67 Elegant, neoclassical arches grace the facade of this lovely church built by Michelozzo.

Santa Maria Novella ▷ 66 A great Dominican church with an exquisite facade.

Santa Croce ▷ 33 The largest Franciscan church in Italy, incorporating the Cappella dei Pazzi. Galileo and Michelangelo are buried here.

San Miniato al Monte ▷ 83 A fine Romanesque church perched on a hill with wonderful views.

San Marco ▷ 65 Beautiful convent where the paintings of Fra Angelico are a feast for the eyes.

San Lorenzo ▷ 64 This church is a superb example of archetypal Renaissance architecture.

Ponte Vecchio ▷ 34–35 One of the immediately recognizable emblems of Florence.

Piazza della Signoria ▷ 32 A traffic-free open-air sculpture gallery surrounded by elegant cafés.

These pages are a quick guide to the Top 25, which are described in more detail later. Here they are listed alphabetically, and the tinted background shows which area they are in.

Cappella Brancacci ▷ 81 The chapel is covered from top to bottom with a monumental fresco cycle.

Cappella dei Pazzi ▷ 26 An early Renaissance masterpiece by Filippo Brunelleschi.

Cappelle Medicee ▷ 57 The Medici family's tombs and private chapels, visible proof of their wealth.

Duomo ▷ 58–59 A sublime masterpiece of Renaissance architecture topped by a mighty dome.

Fiesole ▷ 97 The perfect hilltop destination for a change from the city and its crowds.

Galleria dell'Accademia ▷ 60–61 Home to *David*, Michelangelo's world-famous sculpture.

Galleria degli Uffizi ▷ 28–29 The most important collection of Renaissance art anywhere.

Giardino di Boboli ▷ 82 A green space in the middle of Florence and a cool oasis on a hot summer's day.

Museo Galileo ▷ 27 The history of science brought to life with this fine collection.

Museo dell'Opera del Duomo ▷ 62 Museum housing sculpture from the Duomo and Baptistery.

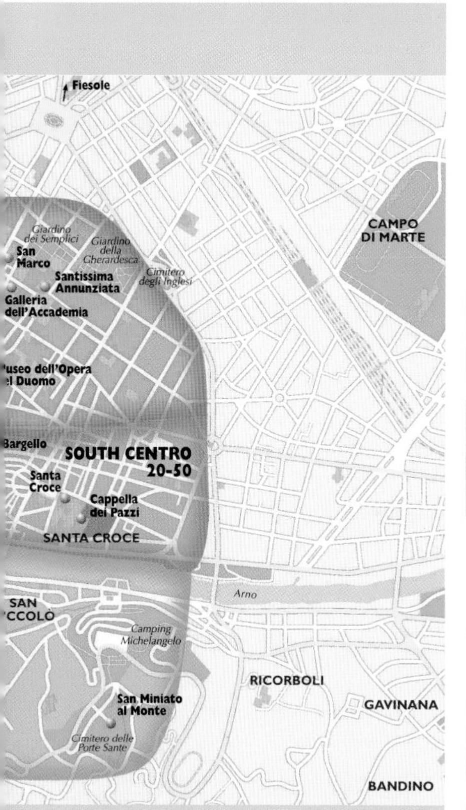

Palazzo Vecchio ▷ 30 The grand 14th-century embodiment of Florentine civic purposes.

Palazzo Pitti ▷ 84–85 The city's largest and most opulent palace, containing a fine picture collection.

Palazzo Medici-Riccardi ▷ 63 The residence of the Medici until 1540.

Shopping

Florence may be small, but its shopping scene packs a punch. This little city has it all and holds an advantage over larger rivals Milan and Rome in that it is easily accessible on foot. Italians and visitors alike dive into the heady mix of chic designer stores and bargain market stalls, quirky boutiques, independent fashion ateliers and artisan workshops. Gastronomes will be impressed by the variety of food and wine on offer at rival outlets Eataly (▷ 72) and the top floor of the Mercato Centrale (▷ 68), converted in 2015, but also intrigued by tiny grocer's shops and *gastronomie* (delicatessen) in residential neighborhoods where the locals do their daily shopping.

Something to Take Home

The nicest souvenirs are often everyday items—kitchenware, household linen, tools and stationery. Head for the San Lorenzo market area for good-value espresso coffee-makers and the tiny cups to go with them, wonderful gadgets such as fish-scalers, and plastic utensils in vivid shades. Inexpensive, cheerful children's toys also make good gifts; the tiny shops away from the main streets often offer the best value. Fresh produce and leather goods are also in plentiful supply in Florence's markets. Food is a popular take-home; aside from expensive olive oil and local wine, don't overlook more prosaic items such as dried herbs specially blended for different foods, the excellent stock cubes known as *dadi* or sachets of vanilla sugar.

STREET TRADE

Street trading is part of the Florentine scene, as in all major Italian cities, with tourists being offered everything from fake designer bags to African objects. However, most traders are unlicensed and keep a constant eye open for approaching *carabinieri*, ready to scoop up their merchandise and run. Be aware the authorities take a dim view of such practices and purchasers can be heavily fined for buying counterfeit goods.

Florence is the place to shop for shoes, designer names, leather goods and culinary delights

Something to take home—a designer garment from Pucci, local produce or Florentine paper

Traditional Crafts

One of Florence's more unusual attractions is the wealth of artisan workshops, clustered mainly across the river in the bohemian Oltrarno area. Many specialize in antiques restoration for the city's numerous dealers, but there are others engaging in more everyday activities. Look for picture framers where you can get new purchases mounted, shoemakers selling wonderful velvet pads and brushes, and book binders where you may have a chance to watch the whole creative process.

Florence on View

Prints, books and old maps and city plans make special souvenirs. Another good option is a cookbook on Tuscan cuisine, which are readily available in English. Beautiful calendars with views of Florence are on sale as early as April for the following year. The museum shops are good for these, too. Via Maggio and Via de' Fossi are lined with venerable antiques shops with interesting treasures in the windows.

Florentine Kitsch

There's no chance that you'll be overwhelmed by good taste either; there are T-shirts bearing images of Michelangelo and Botticelli, plastic models of the Duomo and Ponte Vecchio, umbrellas shaped like the Duomo, grotesque ceramics and fakes of every description. Where else could you buy such a garish silvery reproduction of Michelangelo's *David*, complete with twinkling lights?

ON A BUDGET

Markets are the best source of inexpensive and second-hand clothing. The Cascine market (▷ 98), held each Tuesday morning, is where locals go for bargains. The area around San Lorenzo is a great place for up-to-the-minute, inexpensive designs. The Mall (☎ 055 865 7775; themall.it), a 30-minute drive south of Florence at Leccio, has outlets for all the major top designer brands (twice daily bus service from Florence central bus station).

Shopping by Theme

For a more detailed write-up of these shops, see Florence by Area.

Antiques and Prints
Antichità Monna Agnese (▷ 102)
Baccani (▷ 41)
Bartolozzi & Maioli (▷ 89)
Bottega delle Stampe (▷ 89)
La Casa della Stampa (▷ 89)
Cornici Campani (▷ 71)
Vanda Nencioni (▷ 45)

Ceramics and Homeware
Armando Poggi (▷ 41)
Arte Creta (▷ 71)
Bartolini (▷ 71)
La Botteghina del Ceramista (▷ 71)
Ceramiche Artistiche Santa Caterina (▷ 102)
Ceramisti d'Arté (▷ 101)
Moleria Locchi (▷ 90)
Pampaloni (▷ 44)
Richard Ginori (▷ 73)
Sbigoli Terrecotte (▷ 73)

Department Stores
Coin (▷ 42)
La Rinascente (▷ 44)

Fashion
Anichini (▷ 41)
Anna (▷ 89)
Emilio Cavallini (▷ 42)
Emilio Pucci (▷ 42)
Intimissimi (▷ 72)
J. T. Casini ▷ (90)
Luisa Via Roma (▷ 43)
Roberto Cavalli (▷ 45)
Trame di Storia (▷ 102)

Food and Drink
Alessi (▷ 71)
Bacchus Enoteca (▷ 101)
Caniparoli (▷ 101)
Casa del Vino (▷ 71)
Drogheria Manganelli (▷ 102)
Eataly (▷ 72)
Enoteca Marsili (▷ 101)
Enoteca Peri (▷ 89)
Federico Salza (▷ 101)
Mercato del Carmine (▷ 101)
Morbidi (▷ 102)
Olio & Convivium (▷ 90)
Olivia (▷ 92)
Osteria de l'Ortolano (▷ 72)
Pegna (▷ 44)
Sforno (▷ 90)
Taddeucci (▷ 101)
Vestri (▷ 73)
Zanobini (▷ 73)

Jewellery
Angela Caputi (▷ 41)
Aprosio & Co. (▷ 41)
Cassetti (▷ 41)
Fratelli Piccini (▷ 42)
Parenti (▷ 44)
Penko Bottega Orafa (▷ 73)
Risaliti (▷ 44)

Leather and Shoes
Il Bisonte (▷ 41)
Cellerini (▷ 42)
Furla (▷ 42)
Leather School of Santa Croce (▷ 42)
Madova Gloves (▷ 90)
Martelli (▷ 43)
Misuri (▷ 43)
Otisopse (▷ 43)
Rive Gauche (▷ 90)
Salvatore Ferragamo (▷ 45)
Stefano Bemer (▷ 90)

Linen and Fabrics
Antico Setificio Fiorentino (▷ 89)
Frette (▷ 72)
Loretta Caponi (▷ 72)
Siena Ricama (▷ 102)
Valmar (▷ 45)

Health, Beauty and Perfume
Aquaflor (▷ 41)
Dr Vranjes (▷ 71)
Farmacia Pitti (▷ 89)
Officina Profumo-Farmaceutica di Santa Maria Novella (▷ 43)
Olfattorio (▷ 43)

Stationery, Books and Gifts
Alice's Masks Art Studio (▷ 71)
Feltrinelli (▷ 42)
Giulio Giannini e Figlio (▷ 89)
Letizia Fiorini (▷ 43)
Libreria Antiquaria Gonnelli (▷ 72)
Mandragora Artstore (▷ 72)
Il Papiro (▷ 72)
Parione (▷ 44)
Le Pietre Nell'Arte (▷ 73)
Pineider (▷ 44)
Scarlatti 1896 (▷ 101)
Scriptorium (▷ 73)
Il Torchio (▷ 90)

Florence by Night

After dark enjoy a stroll around the city's illuminated buildings and finish with a drink in a historic bar

To kick off your evening and for a taste of local life don't miss the *passeggiata*. This quintessentially Italian nightly ritual sees the streets thronged with locals, out to see and be seen, while window-shopping, meeting friends and eating *gelato*.

An Evening Stroll

The best place to see the fashion peacocks in their finery is on Via dei Calzaiuoli, linking Piazza del Duomo with Piazza della Signoria. To enjoy a drink while you people-watch, try one of the cafés in Piazza della Repubblica, but be prepared to pay a hefty supplement for sitting outside. After dinner, stroll along the Lungarni, the streets that run beside the river. The Ponte Vecchio is just as crowded by night as by day.

Stunning by Night

Evening is the ideal time to admire Florentine architecture as the floodlighting enhances many buildings. Don't miss the Piazza della Signoria and the area between it and the Duomo. The private palazzi look superb at this time of day and you can peek into courtyards and loggias.

Culture, Concerts and Clubbing

Florence has a year-round schedule of cultural events. The excellent, bi-weekly *The Florentine* is free, in English and has full listings. The monthly *Firenze Spettacolo* also details everything that's on, including rock concerts, clubs and discos, or see a local newspaper.

PICK OF THE PANORAMAS

A great evening vantage point is Piazzale Michelangelo (▷ 87), which gives a glorious panorama of the Duomo illuminated, Florence's twinkling lights and the misty hills beyond. The square draws the crowds during the day but things are quieter at night. There's a restaurant and a couple of bars if you want to spend the evening here, but avoid the park/gardens area below the square at night. In late June, the square hosts the spectacular fireworks display celebrating the feast of San Giovanni.

Where to Eat

Eating is definitely one of life's pleasures in Florence, as it is all over Italy. The food is fresh, seasonal and, above all, local. You'll eat the best of Tuscan produce cooked to Tuscan recipes.

Mealtimes

If you are heading for breakfast in a bar, most open for business around 7–7.30. Restaurants normally open for lunch around 12.30 or 1 and stop serving at 3; they close for the afternoon and reopen for dinner around 7.30. The majority of restaurants have one closing day a week but many open every day in summer.

Trattoria or *Osteria*?

Trattorie are usually family-run places and are generally more basic than restaurants. Sometimes there is no written menu and the waiter will reel off the list of the day's specials. The food and surroundings in a *ristorante* are usually more refined, and prices will reflect this. *Pizzerie* specialize in pizzas, but often serve other dishes as well. Look out for establishments advertising *forno al legno*—a wood-fired oven. *Osterie* can either be old-fashioned places specializing in home-cooked food or extremely elegant, long-established restaurants. All categories will add a bread and cover charge, which will vary from around €2 to a whopping €5 or €6 in the most refined places; a service charge will often be added as well.

Italian cuisine Florentine-style. Nothing beats a drink or an ice cream outside on a sunny piazza

PAYING THE BILL

Pay by requesting the bill (*il conto*), and check to see whether service is included. Scribbled bills on scraps of paper are illegal; if you don't get a proper one, say that you need a receipt (*una recevuta*), which all restaurants, bars and shops are legally obliged to issue. Both they and you can be fined if you do not take this with you. Some smaller establishments expect to be paid in cash but you'll be able to use a credit card in most establishments. Even if service is included, it's customary to leave a small tip—some loose change will do.

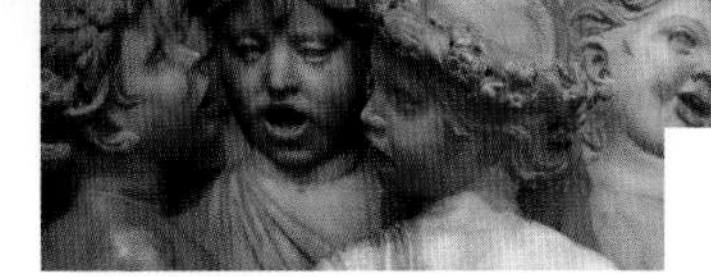

Where to Eat by Cuisine

There are plenty of places to eat to suit all tastes and budgets in Florence. On this page they are listed by cuisine. For a more detailed description of each restaurant, see Florence by Area.

Cafés
Caffè Amerini (⊳ 47)
Gilli (⊳ 48)
Giubbe Rosse (⊳ 49)
Paszkowski (⊳ 49)
Rivoire (⊳ 50)
Robiglio (⊳ 76)

Cheap Eats
Al Tranvai (⊳ 91)
La Casalinga (⊳ 92)
De' Benci (⊳ 48)
Del Fagioli (⊳ 48)
Nerbone (⊳ 76)
Olivia (⊳ 92)
Sergio Gozzi (⊳ 76)

Good for *Bistecca*
Cammillo (⊳ 92)
Le Cave di Maiano (⊳ 105)
Il Fiesolano (Perseus) (⊳ 105)
Il Latini (⊳ 49)

Good for Vegetarians and Pescatarians
Antellesi (⊳ 75)
Belle Donne (⊳ 46)
Burro e Acciughe (⊳ 91)
Da Bruno (⊳ 106)
Santo Spirito (⊳ 92)
La Taverna di San Giuseppe (⊳ 106)
Tre Cristi (⊳ 106)

Gourmet Dining
Belcore (⊳ 75)
Il Cibrèo (⊳ 47)
Enoteca Pinchiorri (⊳ 48)
La Giostra (⊳ 75)
Hostaria Bibendum (⊳ 49)
La Loggia (⊳ 105)
La Ménagère (⊳ 76)
Sabatini (⊳ 76)
Il Santo Bevitore (⊳ 92)
SE.STO on Arno (⊳ 50)
Winter Garden by Caino (⊳ 50)

Ice Cream
Carapina (⊳ 47)
Gelateria Carabé (⊳ 75)
Perché No! (⊳ 49)
Vivoli (⊳ 50)

International
Dim Sum (⊳ 48)
Kome (⊳ 49)
Ruth's (⊳ 76)

Pizza
Baldovino (⊳ 46)
La Bussola (⊳ 47)
Il Pizzaiuolo (⊳ 49)

Typical Tuscan
13 Gobbi (⊳ 46)
Boccadama (⊳ 47)
La Buca (⊳ 106)
Buca di Sant Antonio (⊳ 105)
Cantinetta Antinori (⊳ 75)
Coco Lezzone (⊳ 47)
Da Leo (⊳ 105)
Del Carmine (⊳ 92)
Le Logge (⊳ 106)
Machiavelli (⊳ 105)
Le Mossacce (⊳ 76)
Sostanza (⊳ 50)
Sotto le Fonti (⊳ 106)
Taverna del Bronzino (⊳ 76)
Zà-Zà (⊳ 76)

Wine Bars
Cantinetta dei Verrazzano (⊳ 47)
Coquinarius (⊳ 75)
Dei Frescobaldi (⊳ 48)
Procacci (⊳ 50)
Le Volpi e l'Uva (⊳ 92)

Top Tips For...

These great suggestions will help you tailor your ideal visit to Florence, no matter how you choose to spend your time. Each suggestion has a fuller write-up elsewhere in the book.

EXCLUSIVE SHOPPING

Head to Via de' Tornabuoni (▷ 36) for the best in designer names—Armani, Gucci, Prada and local designer Roberto Cavalli.
All that glitters is indeed gold in the little shops that line the Ponte Vecchio (▷ 34–35), and prices are competitive too.
Florence is famed for its superb shoes, and one of the best brands is Salvatore Ferragamo (▷ 45); you can visit the museum, too (▷ 38).

Typical Florence: designer names and great food

TAKING A SOUVENIR HOME

Stationery—Pineider (▷ 44) has a fabulous array of handmade paper, notebooks and desk accessories. For traditional Florentine paper, try Il Torchio (▷ 90).
Ceramics—choose an authentic jug or plate at Sbigoli Terrecotte (▷ 73).
Wine—Casa del Vino (▷ 71) stocks wines from Tuscany and beyond in all price ranges.

SAMPLING THE LOCAL CUISINE

Sit at a shared table, trying out local dishes, at Il Latini (▷ 49).
The cuisine is Tuscan, the restaurant traditional—try Coco Lezzone (▷ 47) for that classic meal.
Not far from the Duomo, down Via del Proconsolo, try Le Mossacce (▷ 76).

HISTORIC CAFÉS

Giubbe Rosse (▷ 49)—watch the world go by in the Piazza della Repubblica.
Paszkowski (▷ 49)—yet more indulgence on the Piazza della Reppublica—try the fruit tarts.
Rivoire (▷ 50)—in the attractive Piazza della Signoria, it's a perfect spot to unwind.

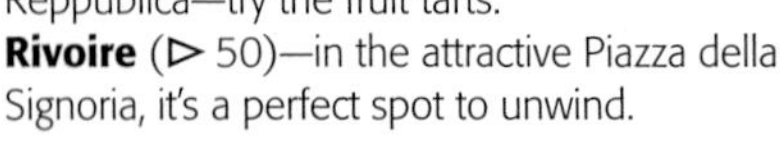

Sample locally made ice cream at Vivoli or skin cream at Officina Profumo

INDULGING IN ICE CREAM

You'll have difficulty deciding what to choose at Perché No! (▷ 49).
For delicious granitas and their special fruity *cremolata* visit Gelateria Carabé (▷ 75).
The most famous gelateria in Florence, Vivoli (▷ 50), changes its specials to suit the seasons.

A ROOM WITH A VIEW

Try the Hermitage (▷ 110) with its roof garden overlooking the River Arno.
For a bird's-eye view of lovely Piazza Santo Spirito and the rooftops of the Oltrarno, head to the beautiful Palazzo Guadagni (▷ 111).
For extreme luxury along with close-up views of the Arno, book into Ferragamo-owned Portrait Firenze (▷ 112).

Florence is known for its stationery—elegant marbled paper products as well as more modern greeting cards

SPLASHING OUT

Stay in the Four Seasons (▷ 112) for sheer luxury and elegance.
Shop in Via de' Tornabuoni (▷ 16) and stock your wardrobe with the top names in design.
Treat yourself to a refined cup of coffee at elegantly retro Gilli (▷ 48).

PUTTING A SMILE ON THE KIDS' FACES

The Museo Stibbert (▷ 98) has a fine collection of armour for your budding knights.
Go to the soccer stadium (▷ 104) to cheer on local team Fiorentina when they're at home.
If you need to cool off, visit the Piscina le Pavoniere (▷ 104) outdoor pool.

FLORENCE ON A BUDGET

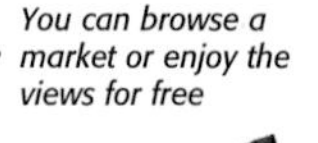

You can browse a market or enjoy the views for free

For good value combined with historic surroundings stay at the Scoti hotel (▷ 109).
If the real thing is a bit pricey, there are great non-designer bargains at San Lorenzo market (▷ 68).
There's no charge to see the stunning paintings in the church of Santa Felicita (▷ 87).

THE CITY BY NIGHT

Sip a cocktail at rooftop SE.STO in the Westin Excelsior (▷ 112).
Take a trip up to Piazzale Michelangelo (▷ 87) to view the city in all its glory at night.
Attend a performance at Florence's modern opera house, the Opera di Firenze (▷ 74).

A LAZY MORNING

Relax over breakfast on the roof garden of a hotel such as the Hermitage (▷ 110).
Amble across to the Boboli Gardens (▷ 82), a cool oasis on a hot summer's day and just the spot for a picnic.
Take refuge in the calm and tranquillity of Santa Maria Maddalena dei Pazzi (▷ 69).

Take a breather in the charming Boboli Gardens

SOMETHING DIFFERENT

Go for a swim in one of Florence's open-air pools (▷ 104), which are usually set in pleasant, grassy surroundings.
Hop on a bus and venture out to see some of Tuscany's hill towns or easily accessible Fiesole (▷ 97).
Be uplifted at a recital in one of Florence's splendid churches such as Santo Stefano al Ponte (▷ 45).

Climb up the Duomo for fabulous views over the city

Florence by Area

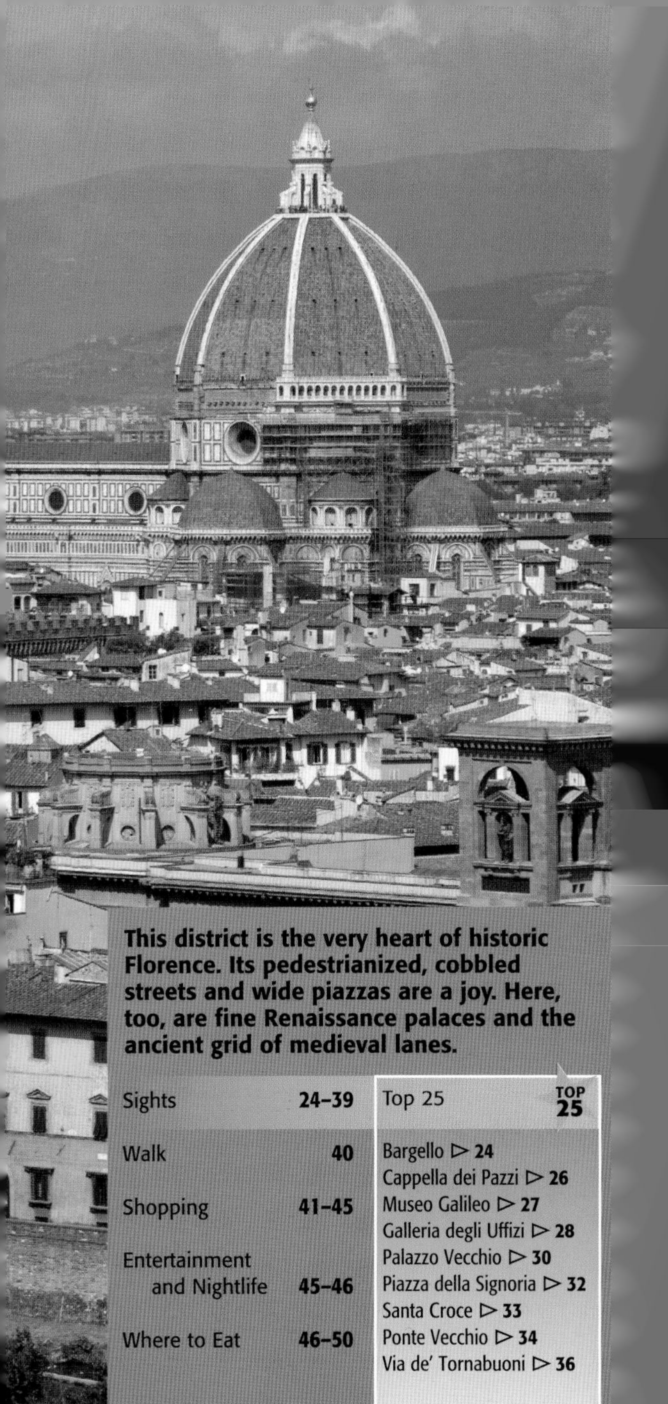

This district is the very heart of historic Florence. Its pedestrianized, cobbled streets and wide piazzas are a joy. Here, too, are fine Renaissance palaces and the ancient grid of medieval lanes.

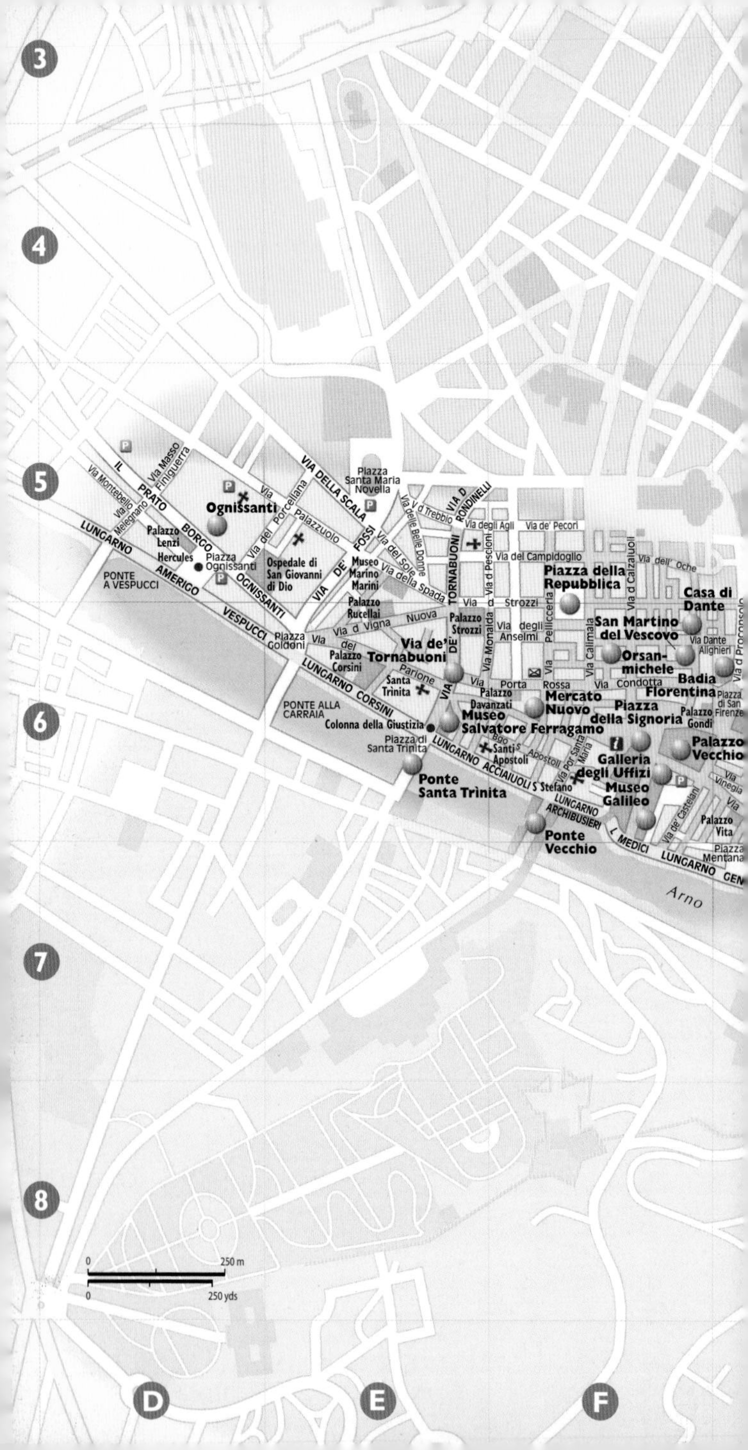
3
4
5
6
7
8
D
E
F
IL PRATO
Via Masso Finiguerra
Via Montebello
Via Melegnano
BORGO OGNISSANTI
Ognissanti
Via Porcellana
Via del Palazzuolo
VIA DELLA SCALA
Piazza Santa Maria Novella
VIA DE' FOSSI
Via delle Belle Donne
V d Trebbio
VIA D RONDINELLI
Via degli Agli
Via de' Pecori
Via del Campidoglio
Via dell' Oche
Piazza della Repubblica
Casa di Dante
LUNGARNO AMERIGO VESPUCCI
Palazzo Lenzi
Hercules
Piazza Ognissanti
Ospedale di San Giovanni di Dio
Museo Marino Marini
Via del Sole
Via della Spada
TORNABUONI
Via d Pescioni
Via d Strozzi
Via d Calzaiuoli
PONTE A VESPUCCI
Palazzo Rucellai
Via d Vigna Nuova
Palazzo Strozzi
Via degli Anselmi
Pellicceria
San Martino del Vescovo
Via Dante Alighieri
Via d Proconsolo
Piazza Goldoni
Via del Palazzo Corsini
Via de' Tornabuoni
Via Monalda
Via Calimala
Orsanmichele
Badia Florentina
LUNGARNO CORSINI
Parione
Santa Trìnita
VIA DE'
Via Porta Rossa
Via Condotta
Palazzo Davanzati
Mercato Nuovo
Piazza di San Firenze
PONTE ALLA CARRAIA
Museo Salvatore Ferragamo
Piazza della Signoria
Palazzo Gondi
Colonna della Giustizia
Piazza di Santa Trìnita
Bgo Santi Apostoli
Via Por Santa Maria
Galleria degli Uffizi
Palazzo Vecchio
LUNGARNO ACCIAIUOLI
S Stefano
Museo Galileo
Via Vinegia
Ponte Santa Trìnita
LUNGARNO ARCHIBUSIERI
Via de' Castellani
Palazzo Vita
Ponte Vecchio
L MEDICI
LUNGARNO GEN
Piazza Mentana
Arno
0
250 m
250 yds

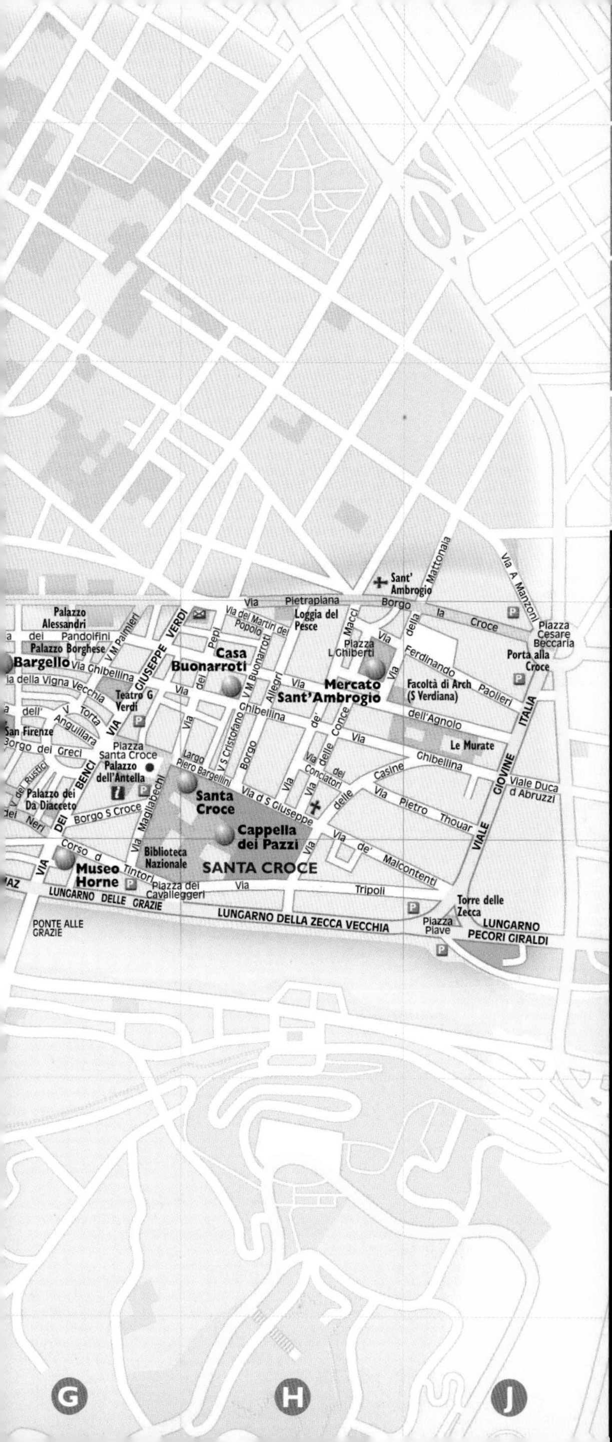

The South Centro

Sant' Ambrogio
Via Mattonaia
Via A Manzoni
Via Pietrapiana
Borgo la Croce
Palazzo Alessandri
Via de' Martiri del Popolo
Loggia del Pesce
Piazza Cesare Beccaria
Porta alla Croce
Via dei Pandolfini
Palazzo Borghese
V M Palmieri
Via Giuseppe Verdi
Via dei Pepi
Casa Buonarroti
V M Buonarroti
Via Macci
Piazza L Ghiberti
Via della Ferdinando Paolieri
Bargello
Via Ghibellina
Via della Vigna Vecchia
Teatro G Verdi
Via Allegri
Mercato Sant'Ambrogio
Facoltà di Arch (S Verdiana)
Via dell'Agnolo
Viale Giovine Italia
V Torta
Via dell'Anguillara
San Firenze
Borgo dei Greci
Piazza Santa Croce
Palazzo dell'Antella
V S Cristofano
Borgo Allegri
Via de' Conce
Via delle Conce
Le Murate
Via dei Conciatori
Via delle Casine
Largo Piero Bargellini
Via Ghibellina
V dei Rustici
Palazzo dei Da Diacceto
Via dei Neri
Via dei Benci
Borgo S Croce
Via Magliabechi
Santa Croce
Via d S Giuseppe
Via Pietro Thouar
Viale Duca d'Abruzzi
Cappella dei Pazzi
Via de' Malcontenti
Corso d Tintori
Museo Horne
Biblioteca Nazionale
SANTA CROCE
Piazza dei Cavalleggeri
Via Tripoli
Lungarno delle Grazie
Torre delle Zecca
Lungarno della Zecca Vecchia
Piazza Piave
Lungarno Pecori Giraldi
Ponte alle Grazie

G
H
J

Bargello

TOP 25

HIGHLIGHTS

- Donatello's *David*
- Giambologna's *Mercury*
- Giambologna's animals
- Michelangelo's *Bacchus*
- Della Robbia's terracottas
- Courtyard

TIP

- The museum is very popular and in high season it is best to book in advance.

The Bargello, with its airy courtyard, is so pleasant that you would want to visit it even if it were not home to what is arguably the finest collection of Renaissance sculpture in the world.

Diverse uses Built in 1255, the Bargello was the first seat of Florence's city government and served as the city's main law court before being passed to the *Bargello* (Chief of Police) in 1574; it was used as a prison until 1859. In 1865 it opened as a museum, focusing on Renaissance sculpture and decorative arts.

Courtyard art The courtyard walls, once the site of executions, carry the coats of arms of the *Podestà* (chief magistrates), whose headquarters were here, and 16th-century sculpture,

Clockwise from left: The Bargello's striking facade up close; the arcaded courtyard; statues line the vaulted walkways; Giambologna's Oceanus

including Giambologna's *Oceanus* from the Boboli Gardens. The ground floor has his *Mercury* (1564) and important works by Michelangelo and Cellini.

Sculpture, medals and bronzes The Salone del Consiglio Generale, a vaulted hall on the first floor, was once the courtroom. It has works by Donatello, including his bronze *David* (*c.*1430–40), dressed in long boots and a jaunty hat, and his *St. George* (1416), sculpted for the exterior of Orsanmichele (▷ 39). On the second floor, enamel terracottas by the della Robbia family include the bust of a boy by Andrea della Robbia. Note the displays of Italian medals and small Renaissance bronzes. The arms room houses ivory-inlay saddles, guns and armour.

THE BASICS

firenzemusei.it
G6
Via del Proconsolo 4
055 294 883
Daily 8.15–2; closed 1st, 3rd, 5th Sun, 2nd, 4th Mon of month
C1, C2
Good
Moderate

Cappella dei Pazzi

TOP 25

The serene cloisters of Cappella dei Pazzi

THE BASICS

H6
Piazza Santa Croce
055 246 6105
Mon–Sat 9–5, Sun 2–5.30
C1, C2, C3
Good
Moderate; joint ticket with Santa Croce and Museo dell'Opera
Access is through Santa Croce

HIGHLIGHTS

- Cloister
- Roundels of the evangelists
- Cimabue's crucifix (13th century)
- Taddeo Gaddi's fresco (1333)
- Donatello's *St. Louis of Toulouse* (1424)
- Museo dell'Opera

The feeling of solitude in the quiet cloisters of Santa Croce (in contrast to the busy church next door) creates a perfect ambience in which to appreciate their grace and harmony.

Convent building On the south side of Santa Croce (▷ 33) are the buildings of a former convent. These include the Cappella dei Pazzi, one of the great architectural masterpieces of the early Renaissance, and a 14th-century refectory, which houses the Museo dell'Opera di Santa Croce. This is one of the lowest-lying areas in Florence, and to the left of the Cappella dei Pazzi a plaque almost 6m (20ft) up shows the high point of the November 1966 floodwaters. The second cloister, a haven of calm, was designed by Filippo Brunelleschi.

The Pazzi Chapel The Cappella, which was commissioned as a chapter house by Andrea dei Pazzi and designed by Brunelleschi (*c.* 1430), is incorporated into the cloisters. This domed chapel is in *pietra serena* (grey sandstone) against a white plaster background, embellished only by terracotta roundels.

Small but beautiful The museum contains many important works, including a restored crucifix by Giovanni Cimabue. On the walls a huge fresco by Taddeo Gaddi shows the Last Supper and Mary Magdalene washing Christ's feet. Prominent is Donatello's gilded bronze statue of St. Louis of Toulouse (1424).

Museum facade (left); the astrolabe of the Gualtiero Arsenio (right)

TOP 25

Museo Galileo

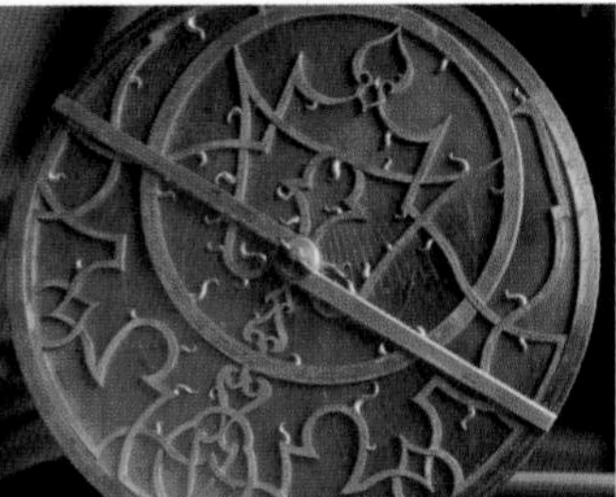

This fascinating museum, with its state-of-the-art themed exhibits, puts Florence and Tuscany firmly among the major players in the development of science. Pick up one of the excellent audio-visual guides to get the best from your visit.

Pure science Focusing on imaginatively displayed scientific and mathematical instruments, the museum traces the role played by Florence in the development of modern science. Its core collection, dating from 1775, was acquired largely by the Medici Grand Dukes and has been displayed in the 14th-century Palazzo Castellani since 1929.

The Medici and Galileo Galilei The role of the Medici, Florence's dynastic ruling family from the 14th to the 18th centuries, in scientific study is appraised via scientific instruments, and there is a fascinating section devoted to maps, globes and navigation. Look out in particular for the sumptuous armillary sphere, used to divine the movements of the planets, made for the Medici in 1590. Pisa-born scientist Galileo (1564–1642) gets star billing, with his telescopes and compasses on display—there is even a reliquary containing his finger bones.

Monumental sundial The giant sundial outside the museum was built in 2007 as a "mathematical ornament." Look for the lizard-viper on the bronze gnomon whose tail shadow indicates midday.

THE BASICS

museogalileo.it
F6
Piazza dei Guidici 1
055 265 311
Daily 9.30–6
C3
Excellent
Expensive
Excellent guide book

HIGHLIGHTS

- Galileo's telescope
- Lopo Homem's map of the world (16th century)
- Antonio Santucci's armillary sphere (1573)
- Copy of Lorenzo della Volpaia's clock of the planets (1593)
- Monumental sundial

Galleria degli Uffizi

TOP 25

HIGHLIGHTS

- The Tribune (room 18)
- Giotto's *Ognissanti Madonna* (1310)
- Botticelli's *Birth of Venus* (1485) and *Primavera* (c.1480)
- Piero della Francesca's *Federico da Montefeltro and Battista Sforza* (1460)
- Leonardo's *Annunciation* (1472–75) and *Adoration of the Magi* (1481)
- Michelangelo's *Holy Family* (1508)
- Titian's *Venus of Urbino* (1538)

TIPS

- Reserve in advance; waiting can be up to 3 hours.
- Plan what you want to see as backtracking is difficult.
- Be patient—highlights are often blocked by large groups.
- There are often long waits for the toilet, so go before you arrive.

The world-famous Uffizi encompasses the artistic developments of the Renaissance period and beyond. It is a powerful expression of Florence's extraordinary role in the history of art.

Medici art The gallery contains part of the Medici's art collection, bequeathed in 1737 by Anna Maria Luisa. The building was designed by Vasari, in the 1560s, as the administrative offices (*uffizi*) of the Grand Duchy.

It's all about paintings Today visitors flock to the Uffizi to admire the greatest collection of Renaissance painting in the world. It is displayed in chronological order and by school, starting with the first stirrings of the Renaissance in the 13th century and ending with works by

Clockwise from left: The Corridoio Vasariano, linking the Uffizi with the Palazzo Pitti, crossing the Ponte Vecchio; crowds gather outside the Uffizi; detail of Filippo Lippi's Madonna with Child and Two Angels; *classical sculptures in the Niobe Room; the gallery seen from the River Arno*

Caravaggio, Rembrandt and Canaletto from the 17th and 18th centuries. Uccello's *Battle of San Romano* (1456) exemplifies the technical advances of the Renaissance, while Filippo Lippi's *Madonna with Child and Two Angels* (c.1465) reveals the emotional focus typical of the period.

Venus Perhaps the most fascinating room is the Tribune, an octagonal chamber with a mother-of-pearl ceiling. In the middle is the Medici *Venus*, whose sensuous derrière earned her the reputation of the sexiest sculpture of the ancient world. Portraits include Bronzino's *Giovanni de Medici* (c.1549), a smiling boy holding a goldfinch. The café provides a welcome pitstop and has superb views of Piazza della Signoria.

THE BASICS

firenzemusei.it

F6

Loggiato degli Uffizi 6

055 238 8651 (reserve ahead to avoid lines by calling 055 294 833 or online at firenzemusei.it)

Tue–Sun 8.15–6.50 (last admission 45 min before closing)

Café

C1, C2

Good

Expensive

Palazzo Vecchio

TOP 25

From left: View from the top; Salone dei Cinquecento; courtyard; striking facade

THE BASICS

museicivicifiorentini.comune.fi.it

F6

Piazza della Signoria

055 276 8325

Apr–Sep Fri–Wed 9am–11pm, Thu 9–2; Oct–Mar Fri–Wed 9–7, Thu 9–2

C1, C2

Good

Expensive

HIGHLIGHTS

- Sala delle Carte
- Sala dei Gigli
- Michelangelo's *Genius of Victory*
- Donatello's *Judith and Holofernes*
- View from the Terrazza di Saturno
- Salone dei Cinquecento

With its fortress-like castellations and its commanding 95m (311ft) bell tower, the Palazzo Vecchio conveys a message of political power supported by solid military strength.

Town hall The Palazzo Vecchio is still Florence's town hall, as it has been since its completion by Arnolfo di Cambio in 1302. Duke Cosimo I made it his palace in 1540, but it became known as the Palazzo Vecchio (Old Palace) when Cosimo transferred his court to the Palazzo Pitti. When Florence was briefly the capital of Italy (1865–70), the building housed the Parliament and Foreign Ministry.

Assembly room The vast Salone dei Cinquecento is 18m (59ft) high and was designed in the 1490s, during the era of the Florentine Republic, as the meeting place of the 500-strong ruling assembly. Vasari painted the military scenes of Florence's victory over Siena and Pisa (1563–65). The theme of Florence's might is underscored by Michelangelo's *Genius of Victory* (1533–34), as well as sculptures of the *Deeds of Hercules* by Vincenzo dei Rossi.

Loggia views On the second floor the Terrazza di Saturno is an open loggia with views to the hills. The Sala dei Gigli is decorated with gold fleurs-de-lys and houses Donatello's *Judith and Holofernes* (1456–60). The Sala delle Carte (Map Room), has a collection of maps painted on leather, showing the world in 1563.

Piazza della Signoria

TOP 25

From left: Neptune sculpture; statue of Duke Cosimo I; Palazzo de Leone

THE BASICS

F6

Piazza della Signoria

C1, C2

Good

HIGHLIGHTS

- Loggia dei Lanzi (1376)
- Cellini's *Perseus* (1554)
- Giambologna's *Rape of the Sabine Women* (1583)
- Ammannati's *Neptune* (1575)
- Rivoire café
- Sorbi newspaper and postcard kiosk

Standing in the Piazza della Signoria in the shadow of the towering Palazzo Vecchio, it is impossible to escape the sense of Florence's past political might.

Political piazza The Piazza della Signoria has been the hub of political life in Florence since the 14th century. It was the scene of great triumphs, such as the return of the Medici in 1530, but also of the Bonfire of the Vanities instigated by Savonarola, who was himself burned at the stake here in 1498, denounced as a heretic by the Inquisition.

Significant sculptures The sculptures here bristle with political connotations, many of them fiercely contradictory. Michelangelo's *David* (the original is in the Accademia) was placed outside the Palazzo Vecchio as a symbol of the Republic's defiance of the Medici. The *Neptune* (1575), by Ammannati, celebrates Medici maritime ambitions, and Giambologna's statue of Duke Cosimo I (1595) the man who brought all of Tuscany under Medici rule. The statue of Perseus holding Medusa's head (1554), by Cellini, is a stark reminder of what happened to those who crossed the Medici. The graceful Loggia dei Lanzi, now an open-air sculpture gallery, was designed by Orcagna in 1376.

Postcard paradise Sorbi, the newspaper kiosk, has a superb collection of postcards and newspapers, which you could enjoy over a drink in the Rivoire café (▷ 50).

Santa Croce's distinctive marble exterior houses many treasures

TOP 25

Santa Croce

Santa Croce is vast yet personal and touchingly intimate, perhaps because of the sense that one somehow knows the people buried here.

Burial place Santa Croce, rebuilt for the Franciscan order in 1294 by Arnolfo di Cambio, is the burial place of the great and the good in Florence. Michelangelo is buried in Santa Croce, as are Rossini, Machiavelli and the Pisa-born Galileo Galilei, who was excommunicated during the Inquisition and was not allowed a Christian burial until 1737, 95 years after his death. There is also a memorial to Dante, whose sarcophagus is empty.

Anglophile The exterior is covered with a polychrome marble facade added in 1863 and paid for by the English benefactor Sir Francis Sloane. It overlooks the Piazza Santa Croce, site of an annual football game in medieval costume.

Artistic riches The artistic wealth in Santa Croce is stunning; frescoes by Gaddi (1380) in the Cappella Maggiore tell the story of the holy cross ("Santa Croce"), and beautiful frescoes by Giotto in the Bardi and Peruzzi chapels show scenes from the lives of St. Francis and St. John the Evangelist. The memorial to 19th-century playwright Giovanni Battista Nicolini, left of the entrance facing the altar, is said to have inspired the *Statue of Liberty*. Santa Croce was severely hit by flooding in 1966, and you can still see a tide mark showing far up on the pillars and walls.

THE BASICS

santacroceopera.it
H6
Piazza Santa Croce
055 246 6105
Mon–Sat 9.30–5, Sun 2–5; closed during services
C1, C2, C3
Good
Expensive

HIGHLIGHTS

- Giotto's frescoes (1320–25)
- Tombs of Michelangelo, Machiavelli, Galileo
- Painted wooden ceiling
- Donatello's *Annunciation* (1435)
- Polychrome marble facade (1863)
- Wooden crucifix by Donatello
- 14th-century windows
- Cappella dei Pazzi (▷ 26)

Ponte Vecchio

TOP 25

HIGHLIGHTS

- Gold and jewellery shops
- Views of the Arno
- *Corridoio Vasariano* (1565)
- Bust of Cellini (1900)

TIP

- The sun sets directly downriver from the bridge, and the golden tones of the structure itself are magical on a good evening.

No visit to Florence is complete without a saunter across this bridge. Lined with old shops jutting precariously over the water, it is difficult to believe you're on a proper bridge and not just a narrow street.

The test of time Near the Roman crossing, the Old Bridge was, until 1218, the only bridge across the Arno in Florence. The current bridge dates from 1345. During World War II, it was the only bridge the Germans did not destroy, though they did demolish the buildings either side. The bridge's luck held again in 1966, when it survived the November flood.

Private path When the Medici moved from the Palazzo Vecchio to the Palazzo Pitti, they decided they needed a connecting route from

Clockwise from left: Ponte Vecchio seen from Ponte Santa Trinita; bust of the sculptor, soldier and goldsmith Benvenuto Cellini guarding the bridge; the Corridoio Vasariano, running along Lungarno Archibusieri, connects the Uffizi to Ponte Vecchio and the Oltrarno

the Uffizi to the Palazzo Pitti on the other side of the river that enabled them to keep out of contact with their people. The result was Vasari's Corridoio Vasariano, built in 1565 above Lungarno Archibusieri and on top of the buildings lining the bridge's eastern parapet.

Glitz Shops have been on the Ponte Vecchio since the 13th century. Initially there were all types—butchers and fishmongers and later tanners, whose industrial waste caused a pretty rank stench. In 1593 Medici Duke Ferdinand I decreed that only goldsmiths and jewellers be allowed on the bridge. As it is a prime tourist destination and one of the places that Florentines regularly come to for the *passeggiata*, it is also always packed and attracts street vendors, hawking fake goods.

THE BASICS

- F6
- C3, D
- Good

Via de' Tornabuoni

TOP 25

History meets style on the smartest street in town

THE BASICS

- E5–E6
- Via de' Tornabuoni
- C2
- Good

HIGHLIGHTS

- Sassetti Chapel frescoes in Santa Trìnita
- Ferragamo shoe museum
- Designer shops
- Palazzo Strozzi
- 17th-century facade of San Gaetano

Florence may be one of the world's richest cultural cities, but it's also a place for serious shopping. Fashionable Via de' Tornabuoni supports the top names in fashion, with chic boutiques vying for space with grand palaces.

Shopping in palaces Italy has always been synonymous with style—think Milan or Rome—but Florence contributes in its own way, too. The city hosted Italy's earliest fashion shows in the 1950s, and innovative designers made their fortunes within the city's medieval palaces here on Via de' Tornabuoni. Salvatore Ferragamo, the flagship store and shoe museum (▷ 38), can be found within the Palazzo Spini Feroni, one of the best-preserved private medieval palaces in Florence; while Guccio Gucci picked this street—three generations ago—for his headquarters, which is still based at 73r Tornabuoni. As you browse, spare a moment to glance up at the facades of the imposing buildings.

Beyond the shops At the north end of the street is the stunning Palazzo Antinori (1465), next to the city's greatest baroque church, San Gaetano (1648), a tranquil spot to escape the crowds. At the south end is Piazza Santa Trìnita, with its artistically rich church. Central to the square is the tall Column of Justice, brought from the Baths of Caracalla in Rome and given to Cosimo I in 1560 by Pope Pius IV. Just beyond here is the Santa Trìnita Bridge (▷ 39), which links elegant Tornabuoni with Oltrarno.

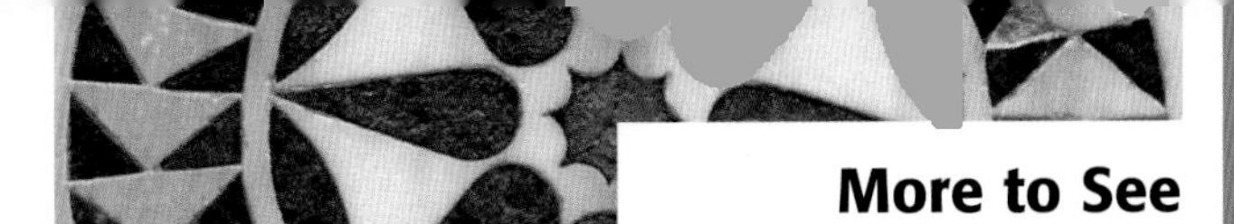

More to See

BADIA FIORENTINA

The Badia Fiorentina, the oldest monastery in Florence, was founded in AD978 by Willa, widow of Umberto, Margrave of Tuscany. It is best known for its connection with the medieval poet Dante, who used to meet Beatrice here. Its magnificent bell tower is Gothic at the top and Romanesque at the base. Inside are two notable works: Filippino Lippi's *The Madonna Appearing to St. Bernard*, left of the entrance, and the tomb of Count Ugo, son of Willa and Umberto, in the left transept.

G6 Via del Proconsolo 055 264 402 Mon 3–6 C2 Impossible Free

CASA BUONARROTI

casabuonarroti.it

This house, which Michelangelo bought in 1508, is now a fascinating museum and gallery. Exhibits include the artist's earliest known work, the *Madonna della Scala* (*c.*1491), a wood and wax model (the only one of its type) of a river god, and a model of the facade for San Lorenzo never executed.

H6 Via Ghibellina 70 055 241 698 or 055 241 752 C2 Mar–Oct Wed–Mon 10–5; Nov–Feb Wed–Mon 10–4. Guided tours can be reserved Poor Expensive

CASA DI DANTE

museocasadidante.it

The 13th-century House of Dante contains material relating to the author's life and work.

F6 Via Santa Margherita 1 055 219 416 Apr–Sep daily 10–6; Oct–Mar Tue–Sun 10–5 C1, C2 None Moderate

MERCATO NUOVO

So-called to distinguish it from the Mercato Vecchio, which closed in the 16th century, this market is famous for the brass boar with a well-stroked nose, *Il Porcellino*.

F6 Loggiato del Porcellino, Via Porta Rossa Mid-Mar to Oct daily 9–8; Nov to mid-Mar Tue–Sun 9–7.30 C1, C2 Good (but crowded)

Mercato Nuovo

Casa di Dante

MERCATO SANT'AMBROGIO

After the Mercato Centrale, this is the second most important market for fresh produce in Florence. It is inexpensive and pleasantly noisy.
H6 Piazza Lorenzo Ghiberti Mon–Sat 7–2 C2, C3 Good

MUSEO HORNE

museohorne.it

This small museum, housed in Palazzo Corsi, owes its existence to English art historian and collector Herbert Percy Horne (1864–1916). Horne bought the palazzo in 1904 for his interesting collection of paintings, furniture and sculpture. On his death, he left the palazzo and its contents to Italy.
G7 Via de Benci 6 055 244 661 Mon–Sat 9–1 23, B, C None Moderate

MUSEO SALVATORE FERRAGAMO

museoferragamo.it

Founded in 1995, this collection of 10,000 pairs of shoes by Ferragamo dates from his return from Hollywood to Florence in 1927. The collection highlights Ferragamo's choice of hues, his imaginative models and experimentation with materials. Many pairs were created for celebrities such as Ava Gardner, Judy Garland and Marilyn Monroe.
E6 Palazzo Spini Feroni, Piazza Santa Trìnita 5r 055 356 2417 Daily 10–7.30 C3, 6 Poor Moderate

OGNISSANTI

This was the parish church of both the Vespucci family and Botticelli's; he was buried here. In the second chapel on the right, facing the altar, is a fresco by Ghirlandaio, which is said to include Amerigo's portrait (the boy behind the Virgin). Ghirlandaio's painting of St. Jerome is also here, opposite Botticelli's St. Augustine in his study. But the real star lies in the convent's *cenacolo* (refectory), where the back wall is covered by Ghirlandaio's magnificent *Last Supper* fresco.

Magnificent frescoes adorn the ceiling and walls of the Ognissanti

D5 Borgo Ognissanti 42 055 239 8700 Daily 7–12.30, 4–8. *Last Supper* in convent Mon, Tue, Sat 9–12 C3, D Poor Free

ORSANMICHELE

Built as a grain market in 1337, Orsanmichele became a church in 1380. The city's guilds commissioned some of the best artists to make statues of patron saints to sit in the canopied niches, and so created a permanent exhibition of 15th-century Florentine sculpture. These statues have now all been removed and replaced by copies; the originals are in the Bargello or Orsanmichele museums.

F6 Via dei Calzaiuoli 055 284 944 Daily 10–5 C1 Good Free

PIAZZA DELLA REPUBBLICA

This grandiose square on the site of the Roman forum dates from the 1870s, after Florence briefly was the capital of Italy. Florentines are not fond of the square's architecture nor its crass neoclassical triumphal arch, but it is a fine open space where you can breathe a little. It's lined with grand cafés and touristy restaurants.

F6 C2 Good

PONTE SANTA TRÌNITA

The finest of Florence's bridges dates back to 1252, although what you see today is a well-executed replica of Ammannati's version, built in 1567 and destroyed by the Nazis in 1944. Ammannati was commissioned by Cosimo I and probably consulted Michelangelo in his designs. Lovely views of Florence, especially the Ponte Vecchio, are to be had from here.

E6 C3, D Good Free

SAN MARTINO DEL VESCOVO

This tiny oratory is set right in the heart of medieval Florence. Don't miss the *lunette* frescoes on the upper walls.

F6 Piazza San Martino, Via Dante Alighieri Mon–Sat 10–12, 3–5 (closed Fri pm) C2 Acceptable Free

Ponte Santa Trinita

Piazza della Repubblica

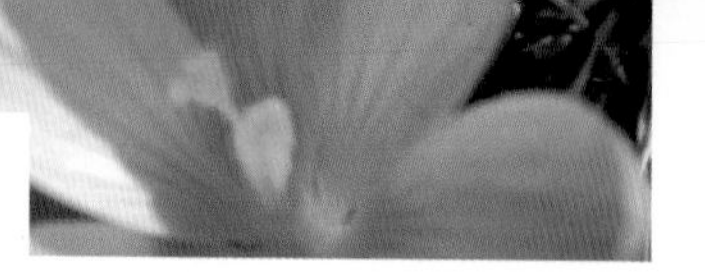

Dante's Florence

A short walk through the district where Dante lived, worked and played, and then on to the eastern part of the city to Sante Croce.

DISTANCE: 1km (0.5 miles) approx **ALLOW:** 1.5 hours including visits

START

BATTISTERO (▷ 55)
F5 C1, C2

❶ Start at the Baptistery (▷ 55), where the poet Dante Alighieri was baptized. At that time, it was not covered with the marble facing that adorns the facade today.

❷ According to tradition Dante watched the construction of the cathedral from the Sasso di Dante, a stone (marked) in the wall between Via dello Studio and Via del Proconsolo, opposite the Duomo.

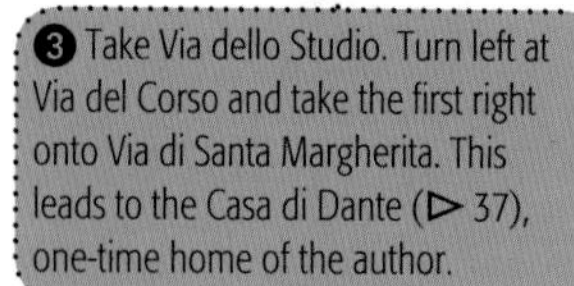

❸ Take Via dello Studio. Turn left at Via del Corso and take the first right onto Via di Santa Margherita. This leads to the Casa di Dante (▷ 37), one-time home of the author.

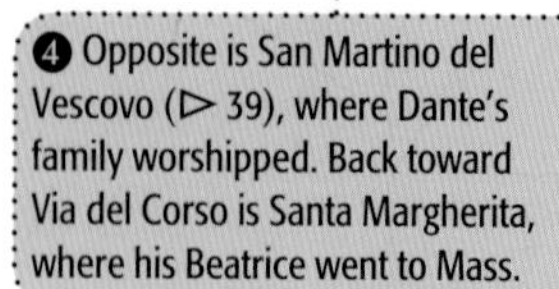

❹ Opposite is San Martino del Vescovo (▷ 39), where Dante's family worshipped. Back toward Via del Corso is Santa Margherita, where his Beatrice went to Mass.

❺ From Santa Margherita turn left onto Via Dante Alighieri for the entrance of the Badia (▷ 37).

❻ Dante often saw Beatrice here and the Badia's bell would have punctuated Dante's daily life. Exit and turn onto Via del Proconsolo, past the Bargello (▷ 24–25), which was being built in Dante's time.

❼ Take the second left, Via dell'Anguillara, to reach Piazza Santa Croce. The streets are dotted with artisans' workshops. Outside the church of Santa Croce (▷ 33) there is a 19th-century statue of Dante.

❽ Dante's sarcophagus, inside the church, is empty. Despite all his connections with the city of Florence, Dante was buried in Ravenna.

SANTA CROCE (▷ 33)

H6 C1, C2, C3

END

Shopping

ANGELA CAPUTI

angelacaputi.com

Angela Caputi is the place to look for bright, bold and highly original costume jewellery. Clothing and accessories to go with the pendant or earrings you have just bought are also stocked. There is another branch at Via Santo Spirito 58r.

F6 Borgo Santi Apostoli 44–46r 055 292 993 C3, D

ANICHINI

anichini.net

The 15th-century Palazzo Ricasoli is the setting for this shop, selling exquisite children's clothing up to age 14 years. Traditional christening robes are trimmed with lace, while for older children there are frilly, smocked frocks, coats, and smart suits for boys.

E6 Via del Parione 59r 055 284 977 C3, D

APROSIO & CO.

aprosio.it

The exquisite pieces in jewellery designer Ornella Aprosio's glittering shop are made entirely from tiny crystal beads. They range from simple items such as bracelets and spherical earrings to intricate belts and evening bags.

E5 Via del Moro 75/77 055 210 127 C2

AQUAFLOR

florenceparfum.it

Master perfumer Sileno Cheloni's shop is located within the vaulted rooms of a Renaissance palazzo. The bespoke perfumes, colognes, soaps, creams, lotions and candles—all produced on site—make wonderful gifts. Try the tomato leaf hand cream.

G6 Via Borgo Santa Croce 6r 055 234 3471 C1, C3

ARMANDO POGGI

apoggi.com

This famous shop stocks one of the widest selections of porcelain in the city, including Giuseppe Armani figurines and Richard Ginori pieces.

F5 Via Calzaiuoli 103r and 116r 055 211 719 C2

BACCANI

This beautiful old shop, established in 1903, stocks handmade picture frames, prints, engravings and old maps. Prices vary from very reasonable to very expensive.

D5 Borgo Ognissanti 22r 055 214 467 C3

IL BISONTE

ilbisonte.com

With everything stamped with the trademark bison, this brand is at the cutting edge of leather bags and accessories.

E6 Via del Parione 31r 055 215 722 C3

CASSETTI

cassetti.it

Maria Grazia's collection of quality jewellery, including period items, has caught

GOLD FACTS

A dazzling array of gold is for sale all over Florence, most notably on the Ponte Vecchio: In 1593 Ferdinand I decreed that only goldsmiths and jewellers should work there and it has remained that way ever since. The gold sold in Florence is 18 carat, often expressed as a rather confusing 750 per cent (with the per cent sign actually referring to 1,000). Gold is also found—at somewhat lower prices—in the Santa Croce area, where, in accordance with tradition, all gold jewellery is sold by weight.

the eye of famous people such as David Bowie, Bill Clinton and Liz Taylor.
F6 Ponte Vecchio 33–52–54r 055 239 6028 C3, D

CELLERINI
cellerini.it
Cellerini offers handmade elegant and sophisticated leather bags of outstanding quality. Styles tend to be wonderfully simple yet cleverly designed.
E5 Via del Sole 9 055 282 533 C2, C3, D

COIN
coin.it
This department store stocks an excellent range of men's and women's clothing, accessories, homeware and cosmetics—all at reasonable prices. The rooftop café has 360-degree views of the city. It is also open on Sundays.
F5 Via dei Calzaiuoli 56r 055 280 531 C2

EMILIO CAVALLINI
emiliocavallini.com
This wacky collection of socks and hosiery is a great source of gifts. Look out for boldly patterned black and white "mantyhose" and "meggings" for the more daring male.
E6 Via della Vigna Nuova 24r 055 238 2789 C3

STYLISH CITY

One of Florence's many claims to fame is as the headquarters of Gucci. It was also in Florence, in 1927, that Salvatore Ferragamo established himself, after having made his reputation in Hollywood crafting shoes for the likes of Greta Garbo, Vivien Leigh and the gladiators in Cecil B. de Mille costume epics. This family still administers a fashion empire, producing accessories and clothes as well as the trademark shoes.

EMILIO PUCCI
emiliopucci.com
This renowned Florentine fashion house was created in 1950 by Marquis Emilio Pucci. The boutique sells his trademark colourful silk shirts, separates, shoes and accessories. Prices are high!
E6 Via de' Tornabuoni 20–22r 055 265 8082 C3

FELTRINELLI
lafeltrinelli.it
Mega bookstore Feltrinelli is particularly strong on art and photography and has an excellent section of titles in English. The café is a good place for a coffee or light meal, and stays open until 11pm.
F5 Piazza della Repubblica 26–29 199 151 173 C2

FRATELLI PICCINI
fratellipiccini.com
If you go jewellery shopping on the Ponte Vecchio, make sure you include Piccini's. They have lovely gold charms, which make a nice gift.
F6 Ponte Vecchio 23r 055 294 768 C3, D

FURLA
furla.com
Furla produces chic leather bags and belts at prices that are less astronomical than elsewhere.
F5 Via Calzaiuoli 10r 055 238 2883 C2

LEATHER SCHOOL OF SANTA CROCE
scuoladelcuoio.com
At the back of Santa Croce church, this workshop sells quality hand-crafted

bags, wallets and accessories at the on-site shop.

G6 Via San Guiseppe 5r (off Piazza Santa Croce) 055 244 533 C1, C2, C3

LETIZIA FIORINI

This beautiful little shop is also the artist's workshop, where she makes charming, and not expensive, handcrafted puppets, dolls and other toys. It's hard to resist buying a Pinocchio puppet or a jack-in-the-box to take home.

E6 Via del Parione 60r 055 216 504 C3

LUISA VIA ROMA

luisaviaroma.com

A popular spot for Florence's image-conscious men and women, Luisa's famous, eye-catching window displays conceal a sleek interior over two floors where well-known labels rub shoulders with in-house designs.

F5 Via Roma 19–21r 055 906 4116 C2

MARTELLI

martelligloves.it

This Florence institution has hand made gloves since 1967 and sells an amazing selection, in every hue and fabric imaginable.

F6 Via Por Santa Maria 18r 055 239 6395 C3, D

MISURI

leatherguild.it

Housed in frescoed Palazzo Antellesi, this is one of the oldest leather factories and shops in the Santa Croce area. Misuri produces top-quality jackets, handbags and briefcases, shoes and small accessories such as lipstick cases.

G6 Piazza Santa Croce 20r 055 240 995 C1, C2, C3

WHAT'S AN ANTIQUE

Under Italian law an antique need not be old, but need only be made of old materials. For this reason, what would be called reproduction elsewhere is called an antique in Italy. Many shops in Florence sell antiques, from the glamorous international emporia on Borgo Ognissanti to the flea market in Piazza dei Ciompi—there are whole streets of them. The most important include Borgo Ognissanti and Via Maggio, for very expensive antiques finely displayed.

OFFICINA PROFUMO-FARMACEUTICA DI SANTA MARIA NOVELLA

smnovella.it

Housed in a 13th-century frescoed chapel, this beautiful pharmacy sells lotions and potions, soaps, perfumes and herbal remedies, still made to recipes handed down from Dominican friars. It's worth dropping in here just to have a look.

D5 Via della Scala 16 055 216 276 C2, D

OLFATTORIO

olfattorio.it

Even if you don't want to buy, take a look at the striking display and interior of this perfumery. Let an expert find the fragrance to suit you, most of which are handmade in France or the UK. There is also a quirky little museum dedicated to early 20th-century powder boxes.

E6 Via de' Tornabuoni 6 055 286 925 C3

OTISOPSE

otisopse.com

Otisopse sells classic leather footwear for men and women at bargain prices

and in a fantastic range of colours; you'll find everything from soft suede moccasins and ballerina pumps to classic brogues and Chelsea boots.
F6 Via Porta Rossa 13r 055 239 6717 C3, D

PAMPALONI
pampaloni.com
This shop is known for its high-quality sterling silver and silver-plated tableware and accessories, and its window displays are often eye-catching and provocative.
F6 Via Porta Rossi 99r 055 289 094 C3, D

PARENTI
parentifirenze.it
Even those who say they're not interested in jewellery end up swooning over Parenti's eclectic mix of styles and shapes, ranging from art nouveau to sheer 1970s glitz.
E6 Via de' Tornabuoni 93r 055 214 438 C3

PARIONE
parione.it
This prestigious stationer's sells hand-decorated marbled paper, personalized stationery and accessories, and also has a collection of beautifully crafted music boxes and miniatures.
E6 Via Parione 10r 055 215 684 C3

PEGNA
pegna.it
This lovely old-fashioned shop, around since 1860, sells its delicious foods supermarket-style. Buy fine cheeses, olive oils, cakes, wines, salamis, chocolates and lots more.
F5 Via dello Studio 8 055 282 701/2 C2

CLOTHES SHOPPING

The most exclusive designers (Emilio Pucci, Prada, Gucci, Cavalli and Armani, among others) are in the district of Via de' Tornabuoni and Via della Vigna Nuova. The area around Piazza della Repubblica and Via dei Calzaiuoli has a good range of major high-street clothes shops, such as MaxMara. In the streets east of Via dei Calzaiuoli there are many mid-range boutiques, while the areas around Santa Croce and San Lorenzo sell bargain fashions to the tourist market.

PINEIDER
pineider.com
Pineider's exclusive stationery and book-binding business was founded in 1774. One of the characteristic papers covering diaries and address books is decorated with great artists' signatures.
F6 Piazza Rucellai 6r 055 284 656 C3

LA RINASCENTE
rinascente.it
This classy department store is stuffed with designer labels for both men and women at good prices. You'll also find perfumery, lingerie and homewares, and there's a wonderful rooftop café with a terrace and magnificent views.
F5 Piazza della Repubblica 1 055 219 113 C2

RISALITI
Quality is assured at this classy jeweller's, and many distinguished clients, including Bette Davis and Ava Gardner, have admired their handcrafted pieces. Their speciality is gold with precious stones in both classic and modern designs.
F6 Ponte Vecchio 27–29r 055 294 656 C3, D

ROBERTO CAVALLI
robertocavalli.com
One of Tuscany's most renowned designers, Cavalli is known for his flamboyant creations. Around the corner is the Cavalli Café Giacosa, where you can relax with a cappuccino and watch the chic Florentine signoras at play.
E6 Via de' Tornabuoni 83r 055 239 6226 C2

SALVATORE FERRAGAMO
salvatoreferragamo.it
Considered to be *the* leading brand in Italian shoes and bags, Salvatore Ferragamo's unique collection is sold in his boutique in historic Palazzo Spini-Feroni, where the poor boy from Naples set up shop in 1927. When you've finished shopping, you can visit the shoe museum around the corner (▷ 38).
E6 Via de' Tornabuoni 4r–14r 055 292 123 C2

VALMAR
valmar-florence.com
This compact shop sells trims and finishings for fashion and upholstery.
F6 Via Porta Rossa 53r 055 284 493 C1, C2, C3

VANDA NENCIONI
nencionistampe.it
This is the place to come for pretty gilded frames, as well as period and modern prints.
F6 Via della Condotta 25r 055 215 345 C1

Entertainment and Nightlife

CHIESA DI SANTO STEFANO AL PONTE
The deconsecrated 11th-century church of Santo Stefano has been converted into an auditorium used for concerts and the occasional theatrical production or exhibition. Schedules are irregular.
F6 Piazza di Santo Stefano 5 055 217 418 C3, D

COLLE BERETO
cafecollebereto.com
Colle Bereto has a sophisticated vibe and a chic clientele who come for pre-dinner cocktails and nibbles. The terrace is a popular spot on sultry summer nights.
F6 Piazza Strozzi 5r 055 283 156 C2

HARRY'S BAR
harrysbarfirenze.it
This American bar, on the banks of the Arno, is a great place for cocktails and has seen its share of celebrity visitors. The international food is also good.
D6 Lungarno Vespucci 22r 055 239 6700 C3, D

MOYO
moyo.it
This buzzy Santa Croce bar has an outdoor terrace and a moody, high-tech interior that fills up at aperitivo time. DJ sets kick in later and it closes at 3am. It's popular during the day too.
G6 Via de' Benci 23r 055 247 9738 C1, C3, D

ODEON CINEHALL

odeoncinehall.it

Housed in the art nouveau Palazzo Strozzino, the cinema has original sculptures, tapestries and a stained-glass cupola. This is the best place in the city for undubbed films in English.

E6 Piazza Strozzi 055 214 068
Times vary. Check the website for schedule
C2

SLOWLY CAFÈ

slowlycafe.com

Chill out to eclectic music at this loft-inspired space, which offers a different sound every evening. The *bella gente* sip classic cocktails while nibbling on Tuscan snacks. It is also open for lunch, and for coffee and cakes from 3pm.

F6 Via Porta Rossa 63r 055 264 5354 C2, C3, D

EVENING STROLL

Going out in Florence in the evening doesn't have to mean actually going anywhere. In summer a really enjoyable and popular way of spending time after dinner is to stroll through the streets of the *centro storico*, stopping off for an ice cream or a drink at a bar. You'll be in good company: Italians of all ages and genders will be doing exactly the same thing.

TEATRO VERDI

teatroverdionline.it

The Teatro Verdi, founded in 1854, puts on drama, ballet and opera from January to April, while the excellent Orchestra della Toscana plays here between December and May.

G6 Via Ghibellina 99 055 212 320
14, 23, C2

Where to Eat

PRICES

Prices are approximate, based on a 3-course meal for one person.

€€€	over €55
€€	€35–€55
€	under €35

13 GOBBI (€€)

casatrattoria.com

Gobbi, with its candlelight and warm atmosphere, provides a romantic setting in which to enjoy traditional Tuscan fare with a lighter touch and tasty desserts.

D5 Via del Porcellana 9r Daily 12.30–3, 7.30–11 055 284 015 C2

BALDOVINO (€€)

baldovinobistrot.com

This bustling trattoria not far from Piazza Santa Croce serves great pizza, cooked in a wood-burning oven, in a relaxed ambience; it's great for kids. The menu ranges from pizzas to salads to *bistecca alla Fiorentina*.

H6 Via San Giuseppe 22r 055 241 773 Daily 11–11 C1, C2, C3

BELLE DONNE (€–€€)

casatrattoria.com

An inexpensive option in an expensive part of town, this modest place offers traditional meat dishes as well as tasty

vegetarian options such as *melanzane alla parmigiana* (aubergine and parmesan bake). You may well end up sharing your table with other customers.
E5 Via delle Belle Donne 16r 055 238 2609 Daily 12–2.30, 7–11 C2

BOCCADAMA (€€)
boccadama.com
Interesting food and good wine, plus views of the Basilica Santa Croce, make this lively historic *enoteca* popular. You can eat outside on the delightful terrace.
G6 Piazza Santa Croce 25–26r 055 243 640 Daily 11–3, 6.30–10.30 C1, C2, C3

LA BUSSOLA (€€)
labussolafirenze.it
La Bussola serves some of the best pizza in town, cooked in a traditional wood-burning oven, plus good seafood dishes. The setting is rustic, the service relaxed, and you can eat perched up at the bar.
F6 Via Porta Rossa 58r 055 293 376 Daily 12–3.30, 6.30–11 C2, C3, D

CAFFÈ AMERINI (€)
Amerini lies in the main designer shopping area and gets very popular in the early afternoon. It serves sandwiches with tasty fillings and good pastries as well as light lunches.
E6 Via della Vigna Nuova 63r 055 284 941 Daily 9–8 C2

CANTINETTA DEI VERRAZZANO (€€)
verrazzano.com
A wonderful wine bar-cum-shop selling breads baked on the premises, this place showcases wines from the Castello di Verrazzano estates near Greve. Don't miss the savoury focaccia baked in the wood-burning ovens.
F6 Via dei Tavolini 18–20r 055 268 590 Mon–Sat 8am–9pm, Sun 10–4.30 C2

CARAPINA (€)
carapina.it
Considered by many cognoscenti to be the best gelateria in Florence, Carapina offers just 16 seasonal flavours at any one time. Look for familiar favourites such as pistachio or stracciatella or experiment with gorgonzola or parmesan.
F6 Via Lambertesca 18r 055 291 128 Tue–Sun 1–7.30 C3, D

IL CIBRÈO (€€€)
edizioniteatrodelsalecibreofirenze.it
This restaurant, one of the city's gastronomic shrines, offers no pasta, but an intriguing range of robust Florentine dishes that vary with the seasons.
H6 Via del Verrocchio 8r 055 234 1100 Tue–Sun 12.50–2.30, 6.50–11.15. Closed Aug C2

COCO LEZZONE (€€€)
cocolezzone.it
Popular with Florentines, with informal white-tiled rooms, this place offers Tuscan classics such as bread- and

ETIQUETTE

Italians have a strongly developed sense of how to behave, which applies in restaurants as much as anywhere else. It is bad form to order only one course in any restaurant (if that is what you want, go to a pizzeria). And the concept of a doggy bag could not be more at odds with Italian ideas of eating out—asking for one will result in serious loss of dignity. Italians do not get drunk in public; to do so is to make an appalling impression.

bean-based *ribollita* and rosemary-spiked *arista al forno* (roast pork).
E6 Via del Parioncino 26r 055 287 178 Mon–Sat 12–2.15, 7–10.15. Closed Tue dinner C3

DE' BENCI (€)

osteriadeibenci.it

At this genuine Florentine *osteria* you can start your meal with *crostini* (toasted bread served with liver pate), cheeses and cold meats, then choose from the day's menu, which often includes spaghetti in red wine and a delicious vegetable soup. The meat dishes are particularly good.
G6 Borgo Santa Croce 31r 055 234 4923 Daily 12.30–3.30, 7.30–11. Closed Aug C1, C3

DEI FRESCOBALDI RISTORANTE & WINE BAR (€€)

deifrescobaldi.it

On the corner of Piazza della Signoria, Frescobaldi offers traditional Tuscan cuisine, or the chance to eat tapas-style in the adjacent wine bar. In the main restaurant choose from pasta dishes or substantial grilled meats, complemented by an excellent wine list.
F6 Via de' Magazzini 2–4r 055 284 724 Restaurant daily 12–3.30, 7–11.30. Wine bar daily 12–12 C3

DEL FAGIOLI (€)

A reliable place to sample authentic Florentine home cooking at reasonable prices, wood-panelled Del Fagioli turns out delicious standards such as *ribollita* (bread- and bean-based soup), *bistecca* and *involtini* (thin slices of meat stuffed with ham, cheese and artichokes).
G7 Corso de' Tintori 47r 055 244 285 Mon–Fri 12.30–2.30, 7.30–10.30 C3, D

BREAD

Pane Toscano (typical Tuscan bread) is made without salt. This takes some getting used to, but the blandness makes a good background to highly seasoned foods such as the Florentine salami *Finocchiona*, which is scented with fennel and garlic. And the bread's texture—firm, almost coarse, and very substantial—is wonderful. Strict laws govern what goes into Italian bread: It is free of chemical preservatives.

DIM SUM (€)

dimsumrestaurant.it

A refreshing change after all that rustic Florentine food, this contemporary dim sum restaurant makes its own noodles. The steamed dumplings are also delicious. Lunch is a particular bargain.
G6 Via de' Neri 37r 055 284 331 Tue–Sun 12–3, 7–11 C1, C3, D

ENOTECA PINCHIORRI (€€€)

enotecapinchiorri.it

Set in a Renaissance palazzo with a delightful courtyard, this celebrated temple to Italian cuisine is one of only a handful of three Michelin-starred restaurants in Italy. The ambience is elegant, the creative food superb, the wine list second to none and the service exquisite. Prices are very steep.
G6 Via Ghibellina 87 055 242 757 Tue–Sat 7.30–10 C1, C2, C3

GILLI (€€)

gilli.it

This chic, opulent café in belle epoque style stands on the corner of the Piazza della Repubblica. Stand at the bar for a coffee and excellent pastry, or have a leisurely lunch followed by a lavish ice-cream sundae on the terrace, where prices are much higher.

F5 Piazza della Repubblica 39r 055 213 896 Daily 7.30am–11pm C2

GIUBBE ROSSE (€€)

giubberosse.it

This literary café was once the haunt of the Florentine avant-garde, and the red-jacketed waiters and stylish interiors hint at this illustrious past. Drink coffee and watch the world go by on the piazza.

F5 Piazza della Repubblica 13–14r 055 212 280 Daily 10am–midnight C2

HOSTARIA BIBENDUM (€€€)

hotelhelvetiabristol.com

In the Hotel Helvetia & Bristol (▷ 112), this restaurant and cocktail bar exudes exclusivity. Expect gilt, chandeliers, draperies and a formal atmosphere, and a safe but expertly prepared menu.

E5 Via dei Pescioni 8r 055 266 5620 Daily 12.30–2.30, 7.30–10.30 C2

KOME (€€)

komefirenze.it

This popular sushi and BBQ restaurant is housed in a historic palazzo under a gold leaf ceiling. High stools stand alongside a winding counter; whether you sit here or at a table, the tempting sushi train will pass by you. Upstairs you grill your own meat and vegetables at your table.

G6 Via de' Benci 41r 055 200 8009 Daily 12–3, 7.30–11 (sushi till midnight) C1, C3

PIZZA AT ITS BEST

As in every Italian town, pizzas are ubiquitous. Many shops sell *pizza a taglio* (pizza by the slice), which is a good option for a quick and inexpensive snack. In addition to the standard margherita pizza (tomato, mozzarella and basil), you will find all kinds of other delicious toppings, such as zucchini flowers and artichokes.

IL LATINI (€€)

illatini.com

This lively, informal restaurant, where you are likely to share a communal table, offers Tuscan classics such as *zuppa di fagioli* (bean soup) and one of the biggest T-bone steaks you'll ever see. Meat is a speciality.

E5 Via dei Palchetti 6r 055 210 916 Tue–Sun 12.30–2, 7–10.30 C1, C3

PASZKOWSKI (€€–€€€)

paszkowski.it

On the grandiose Piazza della Repubblica, this is a lovely, if expensive, old-world café and tearoom which is a great spot for people-watching. A piano bar adds a note of refinement.

F5 Piazza della Repubblica 6r Daily 7am–1am 055 210 236 C2

PERCHÉ NO! (€)

percheno.firenze.it

"Why not!" has to be a good name for an ice-cream place. Founded in 1939, this shop still produces plenty of new tastes to get excited about. It is renowned for its *semifreddi*, which come in creamy tastes such as hazelnut mousse and *zuppa inglese* (trifle).

F6 Via dei Tavolini 19r 055 239 8969 Wed–Mon 12–8 C2

IL PIZZAIUOLO (€)

ilpizzaiuolo.com

For great pizza, try this white-tiled restaurant where the Neapolitan-style pizzas (with puffy crusts) are baked in a wood-burning oven. The menu includes pasta dishes and delicious desserts too—try a Neapolitan rum baba.

H6 Via de' Macci 113r 055 241 171 Mon–Sat 12.30–3, 5–midnight C2, C3

PROCACCI (€–€€)

procacci1885.it

This delightful bar is something of a legend because of its *panini tartufati*, sandwiches made with a white truffle puree—just the thing to accompany a glass of prosecco.

E5 Via de' Tornabuoni 64r Mon–Sat 10–9, Sun 11–8 055 211 656 C2

RIVOIRE (€€–€€€)

rivoire.it

This café, opened in the 1870s, is a Florentine institution. At Rivoire, you pay for the view, but it's well worth the money. Set on the Piazza della Signoria, looking out toward the Palazzo Vecchio, this is the ideal place to relax after a hectic visit to the Uffizi.

F6 Piazza della Signoria 5r 055 214 412 Summer Tue–Sun 7.30am–midnight; winter Tue–Sun 7.30am–9pm C1, C3, D

SE.STO ON ARNO (€€€)

sestoonarno.com

All-glass, rooftop SE.STO has 360-degree views over Florence and beyond, making it an ideal setting for a romantic celebration dinner. Marco Lorenzini's sophisticated, French-inspired cooking lives up to the setting with creative menus featuring fish, seafood and game.

D5 Piazza Ognissanti 3 055 271 51 Daily 12.30–2.30, 7.30–10.30 C3

SOSTANZA (€€)

Also known as Il Troia, this ex-butcher's shop is a classic, popular with locals and tourists who all come for the famous *tortino di carciofi* (a kind of artichoke omelette) and chicken breast sautéed in butter. The *bistecca alla Fiorentina* is good too. You may have to share your table with other diners here.

E5 Via del Porcellana 25r 055 212 691 Mon–Fri 12.30–2, 7.30–11 C3, 6, 11

VIVOLI (€)

vivoli.it

Vivoli is legendary; the family have been making ice cream since the 1930s. If you don't mind the wait, the rewards are delicious. There are lots of tempting choices, including an extra creamy *mousse di amaretto,* all served in *coppette* (cups)—Vivoli is strictly a no-cone zone.

G6 Via Isola delle Stinche 7r 055 292 334 Apr–Oct Tue–Sat 7.30am–midnight, Sun 9am–midnight; Nov–Mar Tue–Sat 7.30am–9pm, Sun 9–9 C2

WINTER GARDEN BY CAINO (€€€)

wintergardenbycaino.com

The lavish interior of the restaurant at the grand St. Regis Florence hotel (▷ 112) is a fitting setting for Valeria Piccini's Michelin-starred food. Her well-balanced menus stick close to her Tuscan roots while allowing for a flourish of creativity.

D5 St. Regis Florence, Piazza Ognissanti 1 055 2716 3770 Daily 11–11 C3

STAND OR SIT

You will almost always pay a premium to sit down and to enjoy the privilege of waiter service at coffee shops, cafés and *gelaterie* that often double up as all-round bars to be enjoyed during the day. If you stand, which is less expensive, you are generally not expected to linger too long after finishing your refreshment.

The North Centro

A district abundant with fine churches, the epitome of which is the magnificent Duomo.

2
3
4
5
6
7
D
E
F
VIALE FILIPPO STROZZI
Palazzo dei Congressi
Palazzo Affari
VIA VALFONDA
Via B Cennini
Via Fiume
Via della Fortezza
Via del Pratello
Via C Ridolfi
Via di Barbano
Via C Montanelli
Bettino Ricasoli
Piazza dell' Indipendenza
Ubaldino Peruzzi
Via F Bartolommei
Zanobi
Via delle Ruote
Via Ventisette Aprile
San
Via Santa Reparata
Ex Convento di S Apollonia
Cenacolo di Foligno
Via Nazionale
Via Chiara
Via Panicale
Via S Orsola
VIA GUELFA
Biblioteca Marucelliana
Mercato Centrale
Piazza del Mercato Centrale
Via Taddea
Via Ginori
SAN GIOVANNI
Via Faenza
Via d'Ariento
Borgo la Noce
Via della Stufa
Via del
VIA
Via S Antonino
Cappelle Medicee
Via Canto d Nelli
Via dei
Palazzo Medici-Riccardi
Via dei Gori
Teatro Reg Toscano
Via de' Pucci
SANTA MARIA NOVELLA
V S Cat da Siena
VIA LUIGI ALAMANNI
Obelisco dell' Unita d'Italia
Santa Maria Novella
Piazza dell' Unita Italiana
Via del Melarancio
Via del Giglio
Via d Alloro
Via dei Conti
San Lorenzo
Biblioteca Laurenziana
Mercato San Lorenzo
Borgo S Lorenzo
VIA DE MARTELLI
Teatro Niccolini
Via Palazzuolo
V dell' Albero
VIA DELLA SCALA
VIA PANZANI
Piazza Santa Maria Novella
VIA DEI BANCHI
VIA D RONDINELLI
VIA DE' CERRETANI
Battistero
Duomo
Piazza d S Giovanni
Piazza del Duomo
Via degli Agli
Via de' Pecori
Via Roma
Campanile
Via d Oche
0
250 m
0
250 yds

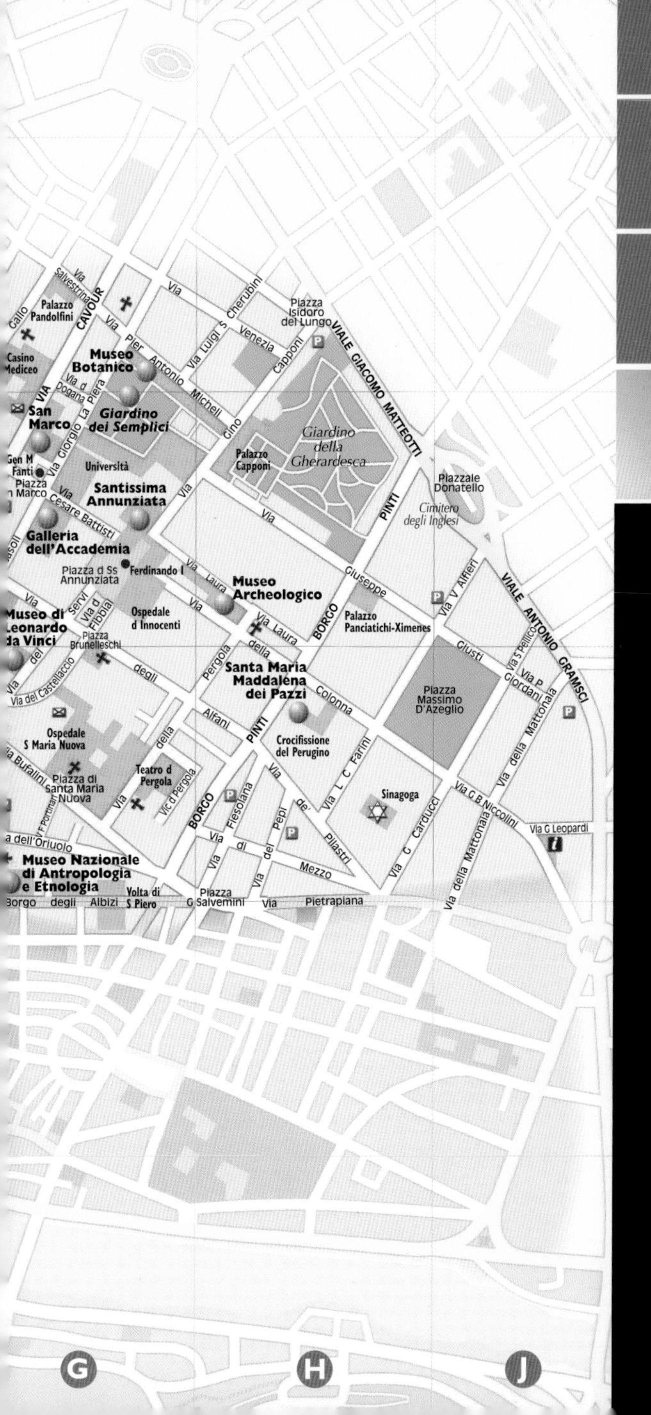

The North Centro

Battistero

TOP 25

HIGHLIGHTS

- 13th-century mosaics of the *Last Judgement*
- Ghiberti's east doors
- Pisano's south doors
- Zodiac pavement
- Romanesque marble exterior

Perhaps the best loved of all Florence's edifices is the beautiful octagonal Baptistery referred to by Dante as his "*bel* San Giovanni," and dedicated to the city's patron saint, St. John the Baptist.

Roman origins The Baptistery is one of the oldest buildings in the city. Remains of a Roman palace lie under it, and the present construction dates from somewhere between the fifth and seventh centuries AD. For many centuries it was the place where Florentines were baptised and it is clear where the font stood until its removal in 1576.

Rich ornament The entire outer surface is covered with beautiful white and green marble, added between the 11th and 13th centuries.

From left: The entire inside of the dome is covered with tiers of intricate 13th-century mosaics, depicting biblical scenes with a large Christ in the centre; the Battistero viewed from the Campanile

Inside, the ceiling is encrusted with stunning mosaics. Above the altar, designs show the Virgin and St. John the Baptist; the main design depicts the *Last Judgement*, with the sinful being devoured by diabolical creatures while the virtuous ascend to heaven. The tessellated floor is almost Islamic in its intricate geometry.

Bronze doors The Baptistery is renowned, above all, for its bronze doors: the south doors, by Pisano (1336), and Ghiberti's north and east doors (1403–24 and 1425–52). The east doors, referred to by Michelangelo as the "Gates of Paradise," are divided into 10 panels depicting Old Testament scenes. In 1990 copies of these doors replaced the originals, which are on view in the Museo dell'Opera del Duomo (▷ 62).

THE BASICS

operaduomo.firenze.it
F5
Piazza San Giovanni
055 230 2885
Apr–Sep Mon–Wed 11.15–7, Thu–Sat 8.30am–11pm, Sun and 1st Sat of month 8.30–2; Oct–Mar Mon–Sat 11.15–7, Sun and 1st Sat of month 8.30–2 (last entrance 30 min before closing).
C1, C2
Good
Moderate; joint ticket with Duomo and Campanile expensive

Campanile

TOP 25

The superb bell tower affords fantastic views of the city—the climb is worth the effort

THE BASICS

operaduomofirenze.it
F5
Piazza del Duomo
055 230 2885
Daily 8.30–7.30 (last admission 40 min before closing)
C1, C2
Non-existent; no elevator, 414 steps
Expensive

HIGHLIGHTS

- Views from the top
- Reliefs by Pisano and della Robbia

Tall and beautifully proportioned, the bell tower of the Duomo is one of the loveliest in Italy and adds a calm and graceful note to the otherwise busy cathedral complex.

Multiple effort The Campanile, or bell tower, of the Duomo rises to 85m (279ft). It was begun in 1334 and finished in 1359. Giotto was involved in its design, but by the time of his death in 1337 only the base was in place. Andrea Pisano completed the second floor and the tower was finished by Francesco Talenti.

Relief sculpture The outer surface is decorated in the same polychrome marble as the Duomo: white marble from Carrara, green marble from Prato and pink marble from the Maremma. Around the bottom are two sets of relief sculptures: The lower tier is in hexagonal panels, the upper tier in diamonds. What you see are in fact copies; the originals have been moved to the Museo dell'Opera del Duomo (▷ 62) to protect them. The reliefs in the hexagonal panels, which were executed by Pisano (although some are believed to have been designed by Giotto), show the Creation of Man, the Arts and the Industries. On the north face are the five Liberal Arts (grammar, philosophy, music, arithmetic and astrology), executed by Luca della Robbia. The upper tier of reliefs, also by Pisano, illustrates the Seven Planets, the Seven Virtues and the Liberal Arts; the Seven Sacraments are attributed to Alberto Arnoldi.

Madonna and Child *by Michelangelo (left); Cappella dei Principi (right)*

TOP 25

Cappelle Medicee

Of all the places in Florence associated with Michelangelo, the Medici Chapels, the mausoleum of the Medici family, are the most intriguing: with tomb sculptures, a *Madonna and Child*, and sketches.

Burial places The mausoleum of the Medici family is in three distinct parts of the church of San Lorenzo (▷ 64): the crypt, the Cappella dei Principi and the Sagrestia Nuova. The crypt was where the bodies of minor members of the dynasty were unceremoniously dumped. Tidied up in the 19th century, it now houses tomb slabs. The Cappella dei Principi has a huge dome by Bernado Buontalenti, begun in 1604 and not completed until the 20th century. The inner surface is decorated in a heavy, grandiose way with the Medici coat of arms everywhere. The tombs of six Medici Grand Dukes are in the chapel beneath the dome.

New Sacristy Right of the altar, the Sagrestia Nuova, built by Michelangelo between 1520 and 1534, is a reminder that the Medici were enlightened patrons. Michelangelo sculpted figures representing *Night and Day*, and *Dawn and Dusk* to adorn the tombs of Lorenzo, Duke of Urbino (1492–1519), and Giuliano, Duke of Nemours (1479–1516). The figure of *Night*, with moon, owl and mask, is one of his finest works. The *Madonna and Child* (1521) is by Michelangelo as well. In a room left of the altar are some superb charcoal drawings found in 1975 and attributed to Michelangelo.

THE BASICS

bargellomusei.beniculturali.it
F5
Piazza Madonna degli Aldobrandini 6
055 294 833
Daily 8.15–1.50 (last admission 30 min before closing); closed 1st, 3rd, 5th Mon and 2nd, 4th Sun of month
C1, C2
Poor; ask for assistance
Expensive
English audio guides (moderate)

HIGHLIGHTS

- Michelangelo's *Night*
- The figure of Lorenzo, Duke of Urbino
- Michelangelo's *Madonna and Child*
- Sketches attributed to Michelangelo
- Charcoal drawings by Michelangelo

Duomo

TOP 25

HIGHLIGHTS

- Brunelleschi's dome
- Santa Reparata remains
- Uccello's mural to a 14th-century Captain-General

TIPS

- You will not be allowed into the Duomo wearing a sleeveless top or skimpy shorts.
- The only way up the Dome is to climb 463 steep, narrow steps—this is not for the claustrophobic.

The famous dome of this cathedral dominates the Florence skyline, with its eight white ribs on a background of terracotta tiles. From close up, the size of the building is overwhelming.

Long-term build The cathedral of Santa Maria del Fiori, the Florence Duomo, is a vast Gothic structure built on the site of the seventh-century church of Santa Reparata, whose remains can be seen in the crypt. It was built at the end of the 13th century, although the colossal dome was not added until the 15th century, and the facade was not finished until the 19th century. The exterior is a decorative riot of pink, white and green marble; by contrast the interior is stark and plain. The clock above the entrance on the west wall inside was designed in 1443

Clockwise from left: The Duomo's distinctive tiled dome dominates Florence's skyline; the highly decorated neo-Gothic facade was completed in 1887; Vasari's frescoes of the Last Judgement*; the crypt has remains from Roman times and the early Christian church of Santa Reparata*

by Paolo Uccello in line with the *ora italica*, according to which the 24th hour of the day ends at sunset.

Roman influences Built by Brunelleschi, who won the competition for its commission in 1418, the dome was made without scaffolding. The best way to see the dome is to climb up it. The route takes you through the interior, where you can see Vasari's much-reviled frescoes of the *Last Judgement* (1572–79), and toward the lantern, from where the views are fantastic.

Explosion At Easter the *Scoppio del Carro*, a traditional costume parade followed by Mass in the Duomo, culminates with a mechanical dove being launched from the high altar along a wire through the entrance, igniting a cart of fireworks.

THE BASICS

operaduomo.firenze.it
F5
Piazza del Duomo
055 230 2885
Cathedral Mon–Wed, Fri 10–5, Thu 10–4 (till 5 Jul–Sep, till 4.30 Nov–Apr), Sat 10–4.45, Sun 1.30–4.45. Dome (access from Porta della Mandoria) Mon–Fri 8.30–7, Sat 8.30–5.40 (last admission 40 min before closing)
C1, C2
Good (access via Porta di Canonica, south side), except for Dome
Free; dome expensive; crypt moderate

Galleria dell'Accademia

TOP 25

HIGHLIGHTS

- Michelangelo's *David*
- Michelangelo's *Prisoners*
- Giambologna's *Rape of the Sabine Women*
- Buonaguida's *Tree of Life*

TIP

- If you want to view *David*, arrive when the museum first opens, or late in the day, to avoid the long lines.

Michelangelo's *David*, exhibited in the Accademia, has a powerful impact: the intensity of his gaze, that assured posture, those huge hands, the anatomical precision of the veins and the muscles.

Art school The Accademia was founded in 1784 to teach techniques of painting, drawing and sculpture. Since 1873 it has housed the world's single most important collection of sculptures by Michelangelo. There are also sculptures by other artists, as well as many paintings, mostly from the Renaissance period.

Masterpiece The main attraction is *David* by Michelangelo, sculpted in 1504 and exhibited outside the Palazzo Vecchio until 1873, when it was transferred to the Accademia to protect it

From far left: Gothic alterpieces from late 14th-century Florence in the upstairs hall; the most famous and most visited of all statues in Florence, Michelangelo's magnificent sculpture of David

from environmental damage. It captures the moment at which the young David contemplates defying the giant Goliath.

Freedom from stone The *Prisoners* (1505) were made for the tomb of Pope Julius II. The title refers to Michelangelo's belief that when he sculpted a statue, he was freeing the figure from the marble, and the style, particularly preferred by Michelangelo, was called the *non finito* (unfinished). After his death, the *Prisoners* were moved to the Grotta Grande in the Boboli Gardens (▷ 82), where the originals were replaced with casts in 1908. Also seek out the original plaster model for *The Rape of the Sabine Women* (1583), Giambologna's last work; the marble version is in the Loggia dei Lanzi in Piazza della Signoria (▷ 32).

THE BASICS

galleriaaccademiafirenze.beniculturali.it

G4

Via Ricasoli 58–60

055 294 883

Tue–Sun 8.15–6.50 (last admission 30 min before closing); closed 1 May

C1, C2

Good

Expensive

Museo dell'Opera del Duomo

TOP 25

Detail of a dancing choir by Lucca della Robbia (left); a fresco in the museum (right)

THE BASICS

operaduomo.firenze.it
G5
Piazza del Duomo 9
055 230 2885
Daily 9–7.30 (Sun until 1.45); closed first Tue of the month
C1, C2
Good
Expensive

HIGHLIGHTS

- Singing galleries
- Original panels from the Campanile
- Michelangelo's *Pietà*
- Original panels from the "Gates of Paradise"
- Donatello's *Maddalena*

There is something very pleasing about the idea of visiting the Cathedral Workshop, the maintenance section of the huge artistic undertaking that the cathedral complex represents.

Refuge from pollution This workshop and museum was founded when the Duomo was built, to maintain the art of the cathedral. Its location was chosen in the 15th century, and it was in its courtyard that Michelangelo sculpted his *David*. Since 1891 it has housed works from the cathedral complex, leaving the Duomo rather empty of art.

Michelangelo's *Pietà* On the first level you can see eight of the original ten bronze panels from the east door of the Baptistery by Lorenzo Ghiberti. On the main landing is the *Pietà* (begun *c.*1550) by Michelangelo. It is said he intended it for his own tomb; the hooded figure of Nicodemus is often interpreted as a self-portrait. The damage to Christ's left leg and arm is believed to have been inflicted by Michelangelo in frustration at his failing skills.

Artists compared The main room on the first floor contains two *cantorie* (singing galleries) that once stood in the Duomo: one by Luca della Robbia (1431–38), the other by Donatello (1433–39). In the room on the left are panels by Pisano from the Campanile (▷ 56); next door are construction materials and instruments used for Brunelleschi's dome.

The Hall of Mirrors has a frescoed ceiling by Luca Giordano (left); the garden (right)

Palazzo Medici-Riccardi

The Medici family ruled Florence with a combination of tyranny and humanity, and this is reflected in the imposing facade of their huge headquarters, with its fearsome lattice of window bars.

Medici origins The Palazzo Medici-Riccardi, now mostly government offices, was the seat of the Medici family from its completion in 1444 until 1540, when Cosimo I moved the Medici residence to the Palazzo Vecchio and this palace was bought by the Riccardi family.

Setting a trend The palace design, by Michelozzo, was widely imitated in Florence, for example in the Palazzo Strozzi and the Palazzo Pitti (▷ 84–85). It is characterized by huge slabs of stone with a rough-hewn, rustic appearance. The courtyard is in a lighter style, with a graceful colonnade and black and white *sgraffito* decoration of medallions, based on the Roman intaglios collected by the Medici and displayed in the Museo degli Argenti (▷ 85).

A regal scene Steps right of the entrance lead to the Cappella dei Magi. This tiny chapel has the dazzling fresco cycle depicting the *Journey of the Magi* (1459–63) that Piero de' Medici commissioned from Gozzoli in memory of the Compagnia dei Magi, a religious organization to which the Medici belonged. Portraits of the Medici are believed to have been incorporated into the characters, while the procession recalls the pageantry of the Compagnia dei Magi.

THE BASICS

palazzo-medici.it
F5
Via Cavour 3
055 276 0340
Thu–Tue 8.30–7 (last admission 6.30)
C1, C2
Entrance on Via Cavour; Cappella poor
Expensive
Entrance to chapel limited to eight visitors every 7 minutes

HIGHLIGHTS

- Gozzoli's fresco cycle of the *Journey of the Magi* (1459–63)
- Courtyard

San Lorenzo

TOP 25

The Basilica di San Lorenzo (left); the cloisters of San Lorenzo (right)

THE BASICS

F5

Piazza San Lorenzo

055 214 042. Biblioteca Laurenziana 055 210 760; bml.firenze.sbn.it

Nov–Feb Mon–Sat 10–5.30; Mar–Oct 1.30–5.30. Biblioteca: Mon, Wed, Fri 8–2, Tue, Thu 8–5.30

C1, C2

Poor

Moderate

HIGHLIGHTS

- Biblioteca Laurenziana (begun 1524)
- Staircase by Michelangelo
- Bronzino's *Martyrdom of St. Lawrence*
- Pulpits by Donatello
- Brunelleschi's Sagrestia Vecchia

San Lorenzo is the parish church and burial place of the Medici and is filled with art commissioned by them. As with the Cappelle Medicee, it is a monument to the family's artistic patronage.

A sacred site San Lorenzo was rebuilt by Filippo Brunelleschi between 1425 and 1446, on the site of one of the city's oldest churches (consecrated in AD393). Its rough-hewn ochre exterior was to have been covered with a facade by Michelangelo. This was never added, but a model is in Casa Buonarroti (▷ 37). A modern statue of Anna Maria Luisa (*d.* 1743), the last of the Medici dynasty, stands rather incongruously at the base of the campanile. The church, with its *pietra serena* (grey sandstone) columns, is cool and airy, with bronze pulpits (*c.* 1460) depicting the Resurrection and scenes from the life of Christ, Donatello's last work. Bronzino's fresco (facing the altar, left), the *Martyrdom of St. Lawrence* (1569), is an absorbing Mannerist study of the human body in various contortions. Inside the Sagrestia Vecchia (Old Sacristy, 1421) are eight *tondi* (circular reliefs) by Donatello depicting the evangelists and scenes from the life of St. John.

Biblioteca Laurenziana The Laurentian Library houses the Medici's collection of manuscripts (not on display). This extraordinary example of Mannerist architecture by Michelangelo is left of the church, up a curvaceous *pietra serena* staircase via the cloisters.

The Annuncication
by Fra Angelico (left); the ornate exterior of San Marco (right)

TOP 25

San Marco

Dominated by the lovely paintings of Fra Angelico, the soothing convent of San Marco has an aura of monastic calm that is conducive to appreciating the religious themes depicted.

Medici motives San Marco was founded in the 13th century by Silvestrine monks. In 1437 Cosimo il Vecchio invited the Dominican monks of Fiesole to move into the convent and had it rebuilt by Michelozzo, a gesture motivated by his guilt for his wealth from banking and by the fact that the Dominicans were useful allies. Ironically, Savonarola, who denounced the decadence of the Medici at the end of the 15th century, came to prominence as the Dominican prior of San Marco.

A feast for the eyes The Chiostro di Sant' Antonino, the cloister through which you enter, is decorated with faded frescoes by Fra Angelico and other Florentine artists. In the Ospizio dei Pellegrini, where pilgrims were cared for, there is a superb collection of paintings by Fra Angelico and his followers. At the top of the staircase on the way to the dormitory is Fra Angelico's *Annunciation* (1440), an image of great tenderness and grace. Each of the 44 monks' cells is adorned with a small fresco by Fra Angelico or one of his assistants. The themes include the *Entombment* (cell 2) and the *Mocking of Christ* (cell 7). Cells 38 and 39 were reserved for Cosimo il Vecchio, who periodically spent time in the monastery.

THE BASICS

polomusealetoscana.beniculturali.it
G4
Piazza San Marco 3
055 294 833
Church daily 7–12, 4–8. Museum Mon–Fri 8.30–1.50, Sat, Sun 8.15–4.50; closed 1st, 3rd, 5th Sun, 2nd, 4th Mon of the month
C1
Acceptable
Moderate

HIGHLIGHTS

- Fra Angelico's cell paintings
- Fra Angelico's *Annunciation*
- Savonarola's cells
- Cosimo il Vecchio's cells

Santa Maria Novella

S-curved volute (left) on the upper part of the facade of Santa Maria Novella (right)

THE BASICS

smn.it
E5
Piazza di Santa Maria Novella
055 219 257
Apr–Sep Sat–Thu 9–7, Fri 11–7; Oct–Mar Sat–Thu 9–5.30, Fri 11–5.30 (last admission 45 min before closing)
5-min walk from the railway station
All buses to train station
Good
Church inexpensive; museum inexpensive

HIGHLIGHTS

- Marble facade
- Masaccio's *Trìnita*
- Cappellone degli Spagnoli
- Tornabuoni Chapel
- Brunelleschi's wooden crucifix (1420) in Cappella Gondi

The decorative marble facade of Tuscany's most important Gothic church incorporates billowing sails (emblem of Alberti's patron, Rucellai) and ostrich feathers (emblem of the Medici).

Dominican origins Santa Maria Novella was built between 1279 and 1357 by Dominican monks. The lower part of the marble facade, Romanesque in style, is believed to be by Fra Jacopo Talenti; the upper part was completed in the 15th century by Leon Battista Alberti.

Deceptive interior Inside, the vast church looks even longer than it is, thanks to the clever spacing of the columns. As you face the altar, on the left-hand side is Masaccio's fresco of the *Trìnita* (c.1428), one of the earliest paintings to demonstrate mastery of perspective. Many of the chapels are named after the church's wealthy patrons. The Strozzi Chapel (left transept) is dedicated to St. Thomas Aquinas and decorated with frescoes (1351–57) depicting *Heaven and Hell*: Dante himself is represented in the *Last Judgement* just behind the altar. The Tornabuoni Chapel contains Ghirlandaio's fresco cycle of the life of St. John the Baptist (1485) in contemporary costume. The Cappellone degli Spagnoli was used by the courtiers of Eleanor of Toledo, wife of Cosimo I. In the frescoes *Triumph of the Doctrine* (c.1365) by Andrea da Firenze, the dogs of God (a pun on Dominican—*domini canes*) are sent to round up lost sheep into the fold of the church.

Detail of Pietro Tacca's fountain (left) in Piazza Santissima Annunziata (right)

TOP 25

Santissima Annunziata

The intimacy and delicate architecture of the Piazza della SS. Annunziata contrast with the grandeur of much of Florence. The roundels of babies on the Ospedale degli Innocenti are quite enchanting.

Old New Year The Feast of the Annunciation on 25 March used to be New Year in the old Florentine calendar, and the church and the square have always played a special role in the life of the city. Every year a fair is still held in the square on that date.

Wedding flowers The church of Santissima Annunziata was built by Michelozzo in 1444–81 on the site of a Servite oratory. Entry is through an atrium known as the Chiostrino dei Voti (1447), which has the air of a rickety greenhouse, though the frescoes inside are superb. The church is dedicated to the Virgin Mary, due to the legend that a painting of the Virgin was started by a monk in 1252 and finished by an angel. Newlyweds have traditionally brought their wedding bouquet to the church to ensure a happy marriage.

Early orphanage The Ospedale degli Innocenti, on the east side of the piazza, was the first orphanage in Europe. A small museum, completely overhauled in 2016, includes works by major artists from the 14th to the 18th centuries. Designed by Brunelleschi in 1419, its graceful portico is decorated with enamel terracotta roundels by della Robbia (1498).

THE BASICS

G4

Piazza della SS. Annunziata

055 266 181; Ospedale 055 203 71

Daily 7.30–12.30, 4–6.30; closed during services. Ospedale daily 10–7

C1

Good

Church free; Ospedale moderate

HIGHLIGHTS

- Andrea della Robbia's roundels
- Facade of the Ospedale degli Innocenti
- Rosso Fiorentino's *Assumption*
- Pontormo's *Visitation*
- Andrea del Sarto's *Birth of the Virgin*

More to See

GIARDINO DEI SEMPLICI

This oasis of neat greenery, the botanical garden of Florence University, is on the site of a garden laid out in 1545–46 for Cosimo I and is named after the medicinal plants (*semplici*) grown here. There are also greenhouses with tropical palms, orchids and citrus fruits.

G4 Via Micheli 3 055 275 7402 Apr to mid-Oct Mon–Tue, Thu–Fri 10–7; mid-Oct to Mar Sat–Sun 10–4 C1 Good Inexpensive

MERCATO CENTRALE

The largest of Florence's produce markets is held in the magnificent cast-iron structure of the Mercato Centrale, built in 1874, with an extra floor added in 1980. In 2015 the top floor was turned into a vibrant food hall showcasing the best of Italian produce.

F4 Via dell'Ariento Ground floor Jul–Aug Mon–Sat 7–2; Sep–Jun Mon–Fri 7–2, Sat 7–5. Top floor daily 10am–midnight All buses to Santa Maria Novella station Good (but crowded)

MERCATO SAN LORENZO

Fun, touristy and centrally located behind the Mercato Centrale and in Via dell'Ariento, this market is known for its bargain leather goods. Much of what you will find is genuinely good value, but keep an eye open for poorer-quality items.

F5 Piazza del Mercato Centrale, Via dell'Ariento Daily 9–7.30 C1, C2 Good

MUSEO ARCHEOLOGICO

This is one of the best places to see Etruscan art. There are also Roman, Greek and Egyptian exhibits. Notable is the rare collection from Kafiri, north Pakistan.

H4 Palazzo della Crocetta, Via della Colonna 36 055 235 75 Tue–Fri 8.30–7, Sat–Mon 8.30–2 C1 Good Moderate

MUSEO BOTANICO

msn.unifi.it

A collection of Florence University, the museum, founded in 1842, houses 4 million specimens—the

Mercato Centrale

largest collection of its kind in Italy. Don't miss the Andrea Cesalpino Herbarium and the superb wax models of plants.
G3 Via La Pira 4 055 275 7462 By appointment only; call first C2 Good Free

MUSEO DI LEONARDO DA VINCI

mostredileonardo.com
This exhibition complex is dedicated to the genius of Leonardo, with some 40 models of his inventions. Categories cover machines connected to the elements of earth, fire, water and air, with a fifth section on mechanical devices. Visitors can have fun manoeuvring the reconstructed machines.
G5 Via dei Servi 66–68 055 282 966 Apr–Oct daily 10–7; Nov–Mar daily 10–6 C1 Good Expensive

MUSEO NAZIONALE DI ANTROPOLOGIA E ETNOLOGIA

msn.unifi.it
Founded in 1869 (part of Florence University), this museum focuses on objects used by peoples from all over the world, ranging from a fabulous ibis feather cloak from South America to rare kimonos from Japan, Inca mummies and trophy skulls from New Guinea.
G5 Palazzo Nonfinito, Via del Proconsolo 12 055 275 6444 Jun–Sep daily 10.30–5.30; Oct–May Mon–Tue, Thu–Fri 9.30–4, Sat–Sun 10–4.30 C1, C2 Good Moderate

SANTA MARIA MADDALENA DEI PAZZI

Although the original church dates from the 13th century, most of the present building was rebuilt at the end of the 15th century, designed by Guiliano da Sangallo. The spectacular interior decoration, with its marble and *trompe l'oeil*, dates from the baroque period. The highlight here is in the fresco of the 1490s by Perugino in the chapter house (reached via the crypt).
H5 Borgo Pinti 58 055 247 8420 Daily 9–12, 4.30–6.30 C2, C3 Poor Inexpensive

Trompe l'oeil *in Santa Maria Maddalena dei Pazzi*

A large painted mummy case in the Museo Archeologico

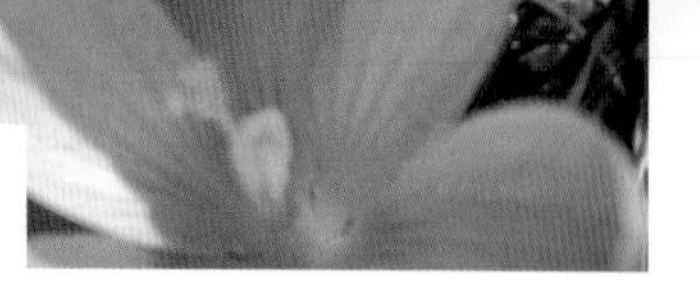

North of the City

Take in Florence's main market area and the most important churches and galleries in the northern part of the city.

DISTANCE: 3km (2 miles) **ALLOW:** Full morning

START

CAPPELLE MEDICEE (▷ 57)
F5 C1

END

SANTISSIMA ANNUNZIATA (▷ 67)
G4 C1

❶ Start at the Cappelle Medicee (▷ 57), in Piazza Madonna degli Aldobrandini, the last resting place of many of the Medici family.

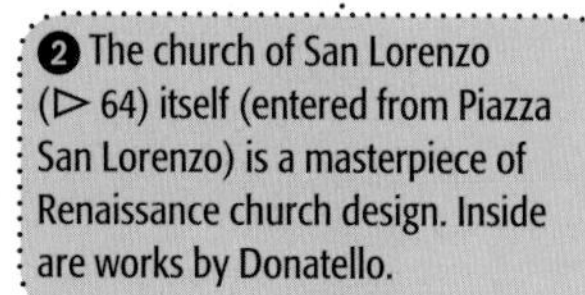

❷ The church of San Lorenzo (▷ 64) itself (entered from Piazza San Lorenzo) is a masterpiece of Renaissance church design. Inside are works by Donatello.

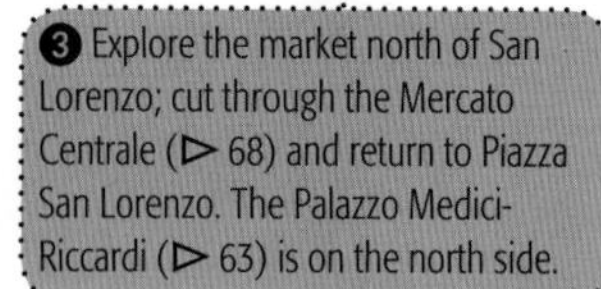

❸ Explore the market north of San Lorenzo; cut through the Mercato Centrale (▷ 68) and return to Piazza San Lorenzo. The Palazzo Medici-Riccardi (▷ 63) is on the north side.

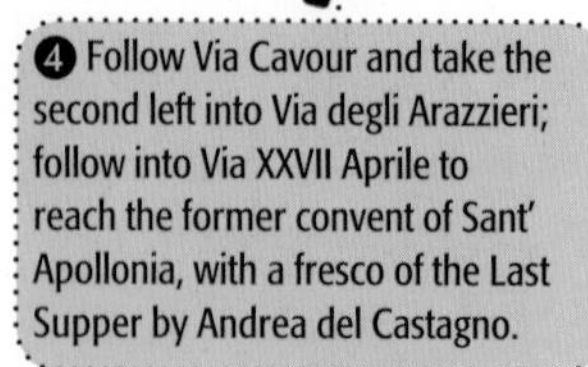

❹ Follow Via Cavour and take the second left into Via degli Arazzieri; follow into Via XXVII Aprile to reach the former convent of Sant' Apollonia, with a fresco of the Last Supper by Andrea del Castagno.

❺ Walk east to Piazza San Marco, viewing Michelangelo's *David* in the Galleria dell'Accademia (▷ 60–61).

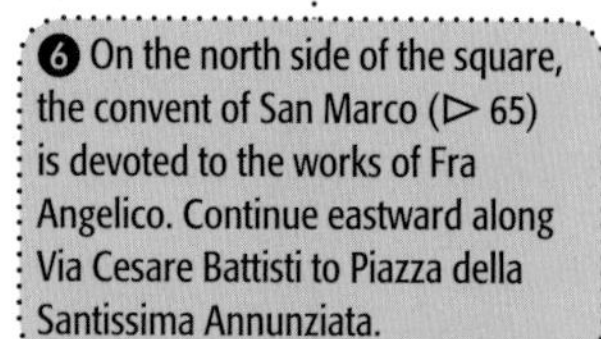

❻ On the north side of the square, the convent of San Marco (▷ 65) is devoted to the works of Fra Angelico. Continue eastward along Via Cesare Battisti to Piazza della Santissima Annunziata.

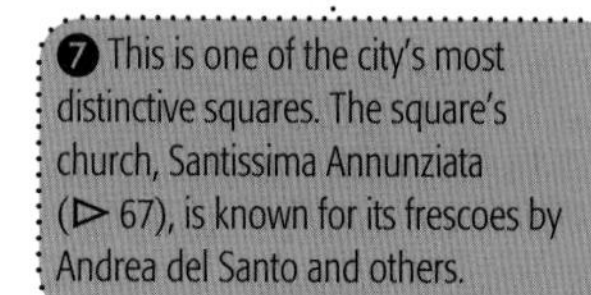

❼ This is one of the city's most distinctive squares. The square's church, Santissima Annunziata (▷ 67), is known for its frescoes by Andrea del Santo and others.

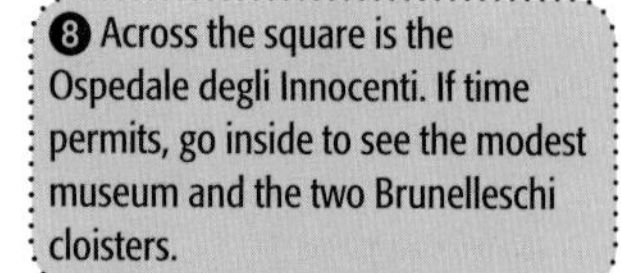

❽ Across the square is the Ospedale degli Innocenti. If time permits, go inside to see the modest museum and the two Brunelleschi cloisters.

Shopping

ALESSI

enotecaalessi.it

With some 2,500 labels to choose from, the Alessi family's shop is an excellent place to stock up on wines from Tuscany and beyond, plus teas and coffees, confectionary, jams and other goodies.

F5 Via delle Oche 27r 055 214 966 C1, C2

ALICE'S MASKS ART STUDIO

alicesmasks.weebly.com

Papier-mâché in all shapes and sizes is here: animals—mythical and real—as well as more theatrical and surreal characters. They are all hand painted and finished.

E4 Via Faenza 72r 055 287 370 C2

ARTE CRETA

Admire artist Elisabetta di Costanzo painting her majolica fresh from the kiln in brilliant hues. Her delightful pieces make a refreshing souvenir.

G6 Via del Proconsolo 63r 055 284 341 C1, C2

BARTOLINI

dinobartolini.it

This Florentine institution sells just about every item of kitchenware you could wish for, as well as fine china and porcelain. All the international names are here but look out for the Italian ceramics such as Solimene-Vietri ware.

G5 Via dei Servi 72r 055 291 497 C1

LA BOTTEGHINA DEL CERAMISTA

labotteghinadelceramista.it

The vivid patterns that are hand painted on the jugs, bowls and dishes at this shop will brighten any table.

F4 Via Guelfa 5r 055 287 367 C2, D

CASA DEL VINO

casadelvino.it

This wine shop has occupied the same premises since it first opened in the second half of the 19th century. Today it has a very well-stocked cellar with nearly 1,000 wines from around the world. You are invited to sample wine by the glass and have a snack while deciding which bottle to buy.

F4 Via dell'Ariento 16r 055 215 609 C2, D

CORNICI CAMPANI

This artisan shop has been dedicated to handcrafting picture frames since 1889. The founder, Gino Campani, was a well-known collector and celebrated frame maker. Custom-made frames take approximately one week to complete, and they won't come cheap.

G5 Via dei Servi 22r 055 216 984 C1

DR VRANJES

drvranjes.it

Best known for his room scents, which come presented in beautiful glass bottles with names such as "Air," "Ginger Lime," "Pomegranate" and "Boboli Gardens," Paolo Vranjes has several shops in Florence. His candles, body lotions and bath oils are delicious too.

G3 Via San Gallo 63 055 494 537 C1, 1, 11

MARBLED PAPER

The skill of marbling paper was brought to Florence from Venice, where it had been learned from the East in the 12th century. Today's Florentine paper goods range greatly in price and quality, but even the inexpensive goods are attractive—and easily transported.

EATALY

eataly.net

The Florence branch of Eataly, the food emporium that showcases the very best of Italian produce, offers an incredible assortment of pasta, cheeses, cured meats, olive oils and vinegars, sweets and wines. It's open daily until 10.30.

F5 Via Martelli 22r 055 015 360 C1

FRETTE

frette.com

This world-famous Italian company produces refined fabrics for the home, always at the cutting edge of fashion—bedding, tableware and lots more.

G4 Via Cavour 2r 055 211 369 C1

INTIMISSIMI

The simple cotton and silk lingerie and sleepwear is hard to beat in terms of quality and price.

E5 Via de Cerretani 15r 055 239 9132 C2

LIBRERIA ANTIQUARIA GONNELLI

gonnelli.it

For more than a century collectors have been coming to this historic bookshop to discover old and rare books, stamps and manuscripts.

G4 Via Ricasoli 14r 055 216 835 C1, C2

LORETTA CAPONI

lorettacaponi.com

Loretta Caponi's store is filled with hand-embroidered table linens, nightclothes and lingerie for mother and daughter, and silk pyjamas for men. It's a good source of wedding presents.

E5 Piazza Antinori 4r 055 213 668 C2

SHOE CITY

The Florentines are famed for making superb shoes. As a testament to the historical importance of the industry in the city's economy, one of the main streets in Florence is named after the shoemakers (Calzaiuoli). The range of shoes available is vast, from the pinnacle of international chic to the value-for-money styles for sale in the market of San Lorenzo. Showrooms at the leather "factories" in the Santa Croce area are worth a visit.

MANDRAGORA ARTSTORE

mandragora.it

Mandragora stocks an excellent range of arty books, postcards and prints, as well as an above-average selection of gift items such as T-shirts, mugs and calendars. There's a choice for kids, too.

F5 Piazza del Duomo 50r 055 292 559 C1, C2

OSTERIA DE L'ORTOLANO

osteriafirenze.com

A must for fans of Italian food, this excellent delicatessen and catering company has been in business since 1962. Pick up a complete meal to take out or choose from the biscuits, jams and sauces for a delicious souvenir to bring home.

G5 Via degli Alfani 91r 055 239 6466 C2

IL PAPIRO

ilpapirofirenze.eu

These shops (there are several branches) in central Florence sell excellent marbled paper goods in particularly pretty shades. These include little chests of drawers and tiny jewellery boxes.

G4 Via Cavour 49r 055 215 262 C1

PENKO BOTTEGA ORAFA

paolopenko.com

Master goldsmith Paolo Penko makes beautiful jewellery to order using techniques and intricate designs that originate from the Renaissance period. His previous clients range from the Pope to Paris Hilton.

F5 Via Ferdinando Zannetti 14–16r 055 211 661 C1

LE PIETRE NELL'ARTE

scarpellimosaici.it

From this classy shop the Scarpelli family sell beautiful hard and semiprecious stone inlays, interior decorations and artistic objects including sculptures, tables, pictures, brooches and much more. The stones used include onyx, chalcedony, malachite and jasper.

F5 Via Ricasoli 59r 055 212 587 C1, C2

RICHARD GINORI

richardginori1735.com

Florence's own porcelain designer will also make dinner services to order with your family crest, a picture of your home or whatever else you want.

E5 Via Rondinelli 17r 055 210 041 C2

SBIGOLI TERRECOTTE

sbigoliterrecotte.it

Pots here are designed, painted and fired in Florence by the family owners, whose workshop is behind the shop and can be visited. The designs, based mainly on familiar Tuscan themes such as olives or the geometric plants popular in the Renaissance, come in majolica and tactile unglazed terracotta, and at good prices.

G5 Via Sant'Egidio 4r 055 247 9713 C1

SCRIPTORIUM

scriptoriumfirenze.com

This shop draws on two great Florentine crafts—leather working and paper making—to create objects of beauty and refined taste. The plain paper books are notable, bound with soft leather in subdued natural shades.

G5 Via dei Servi 5–7r 055 211 804 C1

VESTRI

vestri.it

Vestri's handmade chocolates come flavoured with chilli, cointreau, green tea, extra virgin olive oil and much more. In winter you can indulge in sinful hot chocolate, in summer chocolate ice cream, maybe with wild strawberries.

G6 Borgo degli Albizi 11r 055 234 0374 C1, C2

ZANOBINI

Part traditional bar, part wine shop, Zanobini's is patronized by locals. Enjoy a snack and a chat with the friendly owners while you buy your wine.

F4 Via Sant'Antonino 47r 055 239 6850 C1

CHIANTI

Chianti gets its name from the region in which it is made. Sangiovese grapes are harvested in October, pressed and then the juice and skins of the grapes are fermented for about 15 days, after which the juice alone is given a second fermentation. In spring the wine is matured in wooden casks. *Chianti Classico* is usually regarded as the best of the seven types of Chianti. This is produced in the eponymous region north of Siena. Wines of the Chianti Classico Consortium bear the symbol of the Gallo Nero (black cockerel).

Entertainment and Nightlife

JAZZ CLUB

Jazz aficionados flock to this popular venue for its programme of live jazz and relaxed atmosphere. Although technically a private club, it is very easy to become a member (▷ panel).
H5 Via Nuova dei Caccini 3 055 527 1815 Closed Mon, Sun and Jun–Sep C1

LYCEUM

lyceumclubfirenze.net
The Lyceum presents an occasional schedule of chamber music and classical recitals in elegant surroundings.
G5 Via degli Alfani 48r 055 247 8264 C1, C2

OPERA DI FIRENZE

operadifirenze.it
Florence's spectacular modern opera house, with its 2,000-seater auditorium, is the main venue of the Maggio Musicale music festival in May and June, but has a full programme of opera, concerts and dance throughout the year.
C5 Via Vittorio Gui 1 Box office 055 277 9309 C1, C2, D

CLUBS ITALIAN STYLE

Many clubs and music venues are private clubs or *associazione culturale*. This doesn't mean that visitors are unwelcome but that it's easier for them to get a licence as a club than as a public *locale*. It's very easy to become a member; you may be charged a euro or so above the official entry price, but it's still worth doing even if you're only going to use your membership once. Many clubs actually have free membership. All you need to do is fill in your name, address, date of birth and sometimes occupation on a form and you'll be presented with a membership card.

OPERA ET GUSTO

This is a novel way to spend an evening, combining a first-class meal with music, dance and theatre. The tables are arranged at the foot of the stage and red velvet curtains encircle the room, creating an intimate, warm feel. After the performance the venue transforms into an open bar with live music.
E5 Via della Scala 17r 055 288 190 Show 8pm–10.45pm. Bar until 2am C2

REX CAFÈ

rexfirenze.com
The stunning interior boasts artistic lighting, a colourful mosaic behind the bar and a life-sized marlin suspended from the ceiling. Great cocktails and good music, both DJ sessions and live, make this place ever-popular, and it stays open until 2.30am.
H5 Via Fiesolana 23r 055 248 0331 C1, C2

SPACE ELECTRONIC

Upstairs you'll find a vast dance floor, where an eclectic selection of music is played, ranging from up-to-the-minute hits to 1950s and 60s classics. It's noisy and very popular with tourists.
D5 Via Palazzuolo 37 055 293 082 D

TEATRO DELLA PERGOLA

teatrodellapergola.com
Internationally renowned musicians are regularly featured on the concert series organized by the Amici della Musica (amicidellamusica.it). Concerts are held either in the glorious red and gold theatre or in the more intimate *saloncino*. This is one of the most important venues for classical music in the city.
G5 Via della Pergola 12–32 055 22641 C1, C2

Where to Eat

PRICES

Prices are approximate, based on a 3-course meal for one person.

€€€ over €55
€€ €35–€55
€ under €35

ANTELLESI (€€)

trattoriaantellesi.com

Antellesi is a great place for a vegetarian to join a meat-eating friend. There's a good range of inventive starters and delicious main courses—the *peposo alla fiorentina* (a peppery beef stew in red wine) is very tasty. There is a decent wine list and a traditional Florentine dessert made with chestnuts.

E4 Via Faenza 9r 055 265 4616 Closed Tue C2

BELCORE (€€)

ristorantebelcore.it

Here you can enjoy refined modern Italian cooking in tranquil, elegant surroundings. The plain cream walls provide a stage for the work of up-and-coming artists. The impressive wine list has more than 300 wines to choose from.

D5 Via dell'Albero 30 055 211 198 Thu–Tue 7–11.30pm C2, D

CANTINETTA ANTINORI (€€€)

cantinetta-antinori.com

Well-heeled tourists and chic Florentines are among the regulars at this elegant restaurant, where the menus are based on classic Florentine and Tuscan dishes such as *pappa al pomodoro*, a typical bread-based tomato soup. Wines are from the world-renowned Antinori estates.

E5 Piazza Antinori 3 055 292 234 Mon–Sat 12–2.30, 7–10.30. Closed Aug C2

COQUINARIUS (€€)

coquinarius.com

This restaurant-cum-wine bar full of dark wood and stylish posters is a great place to sample different cheeses, cold cuts, smoked fish, *stuzzichini* (Italian bar snacks) and exceptionally good cakes.

F5 Via delle Oche 11r 055 230 2153 Daily 12.30–3, 6.30–10.30. Closed Tue Jan–Feb C1

GELATERIA CARABÉ (€)

parocaribe.it

This top-quality Sicilian ice-cream store is *the* place to have a *granita* (ice slush) in Florence, or try the *cremolata* made from the fruit pulp, including melon and blackberry. No artificial ingredients are used.

G4 Via Ricasoli 60r 055 289 476 Daily 10am–midnight C1, C2

LA GIOSTRA (€€€)

ristorantelagiostra.com

Prepare to be spoiled at this enclave of fine dining, owned by the children of a Hapsburg prince. Upon entering, you are offered a crystal flute of *spumante*, which prepares you for the refined menu. The home-made pasta courses are divine and the mains are equally exquisite. Save room for the Viennese *Sachertorte*.

ITALIAN CAKES

There are three main types of Tuscan cake. *Brioche* (breakfast pastries) are made with sweet yeast dough and filled with oozing custard. *Torte* (cakes) tend to be tarts, such as the ubiquitous *torta della nonna* (grandma's cake), a kind of custard tart, or *torta di ricotta*, in which ricotta is mixed with sugar and candied peel. Then there are all kinds of little cookies, most of which contain nuts and have names like *brutti ma buoni* (ugly but good).

G5 Borgo Pinti 12r 055 241 341 Mon–Fri 12.30–2.30, 7–late, Sat–Sun 7–late C1, C2

LA MÉNAGÈRE (€€–€€€)

A café, homeware shop, cocktail bar and restaurant all under the same roof, retro, shabby-chic Ménagère is one of Florence's fashionable dining venues. The food is pan-Mediterranean with the odd creative twist.

F4 Via de' Ginori 8r 055 075 0600 Daily 7am–2am C1

LE MOSSACCE (€–€€)

trattorialemossacce.it

A bustling eatery between the Duomo and the Bargello, Le Mossacce serves excellent Tuscan food, including rich *zuppa Lombarda* soup with beans.

G6 Via del Proconsolo 55r 055 294 361 Mon–Fri 12–2.30, 7–9.30 C1, C2

NERBONE (€)

This colourful food stall has been serving up cheap, rustic food to market workers since 1872. The speciality is *lampredotto* (cow's intestines) served in a bun with bright green salsa verde, but they also offer pasta and roast meats.

F4 Mercato Centrale, Via del Ariento Mon–Sat 7–2 C1

ROBIGLIO (€€)

Old-fashioned Florentine bar/*pasticceria* par excellence, Robiglio's pastries are to die for. There is another branch in Via dei Servi.

F5 Via Tosinghi 11r 055 215 013 Daily 8am–8.30pm C1

RUTH'S (€)

kosheruth.com

This bright, modern Jewish restaurant next to the synagogue serves an interesting mix of vegetarian (and fish), Middle Eastern and kosher food.

H5 Via Farini 2a 055 248 0888 Mon–Thu 12.30–2.30, 7.30–10, Fri 12.30–2.30, Sat 7.30–10 C2, C3

SABATINI (€€€)

ristorantesabatini.it

This elegant, wood-panelled restaurant is a respected Florentine stalwart and particularly good for local steak and xseafood risotto.

E5 Via dei Panzani 9a 055 211 599 Tue–Sun 12.30–2.30, 7.30–10.30 C2

SERGIO GOZZI (€)

This no-frills, lunch-only trattoria has a daily-changing menu of excellent home-cooked Florentine specialities. It lies along the side of San Lorenzo church and is popular with workers from the nearby market.

F5 Piazza San Lorenzo 8r 055 281 941 Mon–Sat 12–3 C2, D

TAVERNA DEL BRONZINO (€€€)

tavernadelbronzino.net

Here you will find a wealth of Tuscan culinary delights such as smoked goose breast with olive oil. If available, try the expertly prepared sea bass.

F3 Via delle Ruote 27r 055 495 220 Mon–Fri 12.30–2.30, 7.30–10.30, Sat 7.30–10.30 C2

ZÀ-ZÀ (€)

trattoriazaza.it

The rustic Tuscan food at this charmingly old-fashioned, inexpensive trattoria near the Mercato Centrale is excellent. Popular with visitors, the inviting stone-walled interior is especially appealing in the summer heat.

F4 Piazza del Mercato Centrale 26r 055 215 411 Daily 11–11 C2

Literally translated as "beyond the Arno," the Oltrarno is the site of the Pitti Palace and the Boboli Gardens. It is also the most relaxed part of the city, least touched by tourism and with some of the best views.

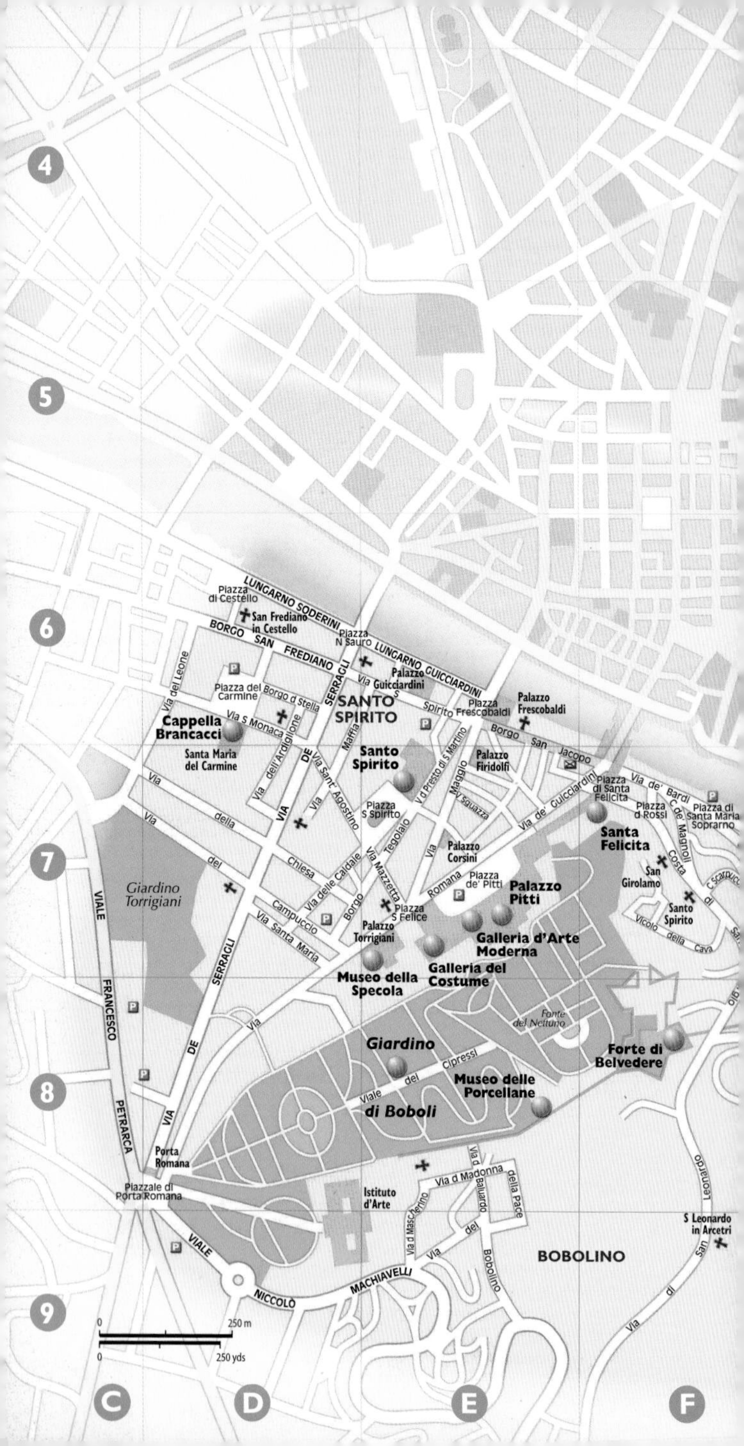

4
5
6
7
8
9
C
D
E
F
LUNGARNO SODERINI
Piazza di Cestello
San Frediano in Cestello
BORGO SAN FREDIANO
Piazza N Sauro
LUNGARNO GUICCIARDINI
Palazzo Guicciardini
Via S Spirito
SANTO SPIRITO
Piazza Frescobaldi
Palazzo Frescobaldi
Borgo San Jacopo
Via del Leone
Piazza del Carmine
Borgo d Stella
Via S Monaca
Cappella Brancacci
Santa Maria del Carmine
Via dell'Ardiglione
VIA DE SERRAGLI
Via Maffia
Via Sant' Agostino
Santo Spirito
Piazza S Spirito
V d Presto di S Martino
Maggio
Palazzo Firidolfi
V Sguazza
Via de' Guicciardini
Piazza di Santa Felicita
Via de' Bardi
Piazza d Rossi
C de' Magnoli
Piazza di Santa Maria Soprarno
Santa Felicita
Costa
San Girolamo
Santo Spirito
Vicolo della Cava
C Scarpuccia
Via della Chiesa
Via del Campuccio
Via Santa Maria
Via delle Caldaie
Tegolaio
Via Mazzetta
Palazzo Corsini
Via Romana
Piazza de' Pitti
Palazzo Pitti
Borgo
Piazza S Felice
Palazzo Torrigiani
Galleria d'Arte Moderna
Galleria del Costume
Museo della Specola
Giardino Torrigiani
VIALE FRANCESCO PETRARCA
Fonte del Nettuno
Forte di Belvedere
Giardino di Boboli
Viale dei Cipressi
Museo delle Porcellane
Porta Romana
Piazzale di Porta Romana
Istituto d'Arte
Via d Madonna della Pace
Via d Ballardo
Via d Maschenino
Via del Bobolino
BOBOLINO
VIALE NICCOLÒ MACHIAVELLI
S Leonardo in Arcetri
Via di San Leonardo
0
250 m
0
250 yds

Ponte alle Grazie
Lungarno Torrigiani
Arno
Ch Tedesca
LUNGARNO
Palazzo Serristori
SERRISTORI
Bardi
Piazza de' Mozzi
Via del Renai
Via del Giardino Serristori
V Lupo
Palazzo Torrigiani
Museo Bardini
Via di
San Niccolò
Niccolò
San
Porta San Niccolò
LUNGARNO BENVENUTO CELLINI
Piazza G Poggi
Via dei Bastioni
Via d Fornace
Palazzi de' Mozzi
SAN NICCOLÒ
V S Miniato
Viale Giuseppe Poggi
Camping Michelangelo
Belvedere
Via di
Via del Monte alle Croci
David
Piazzale Michelangelo
VIALE MICHELANGIOLO
Via di San Miniato al Monte
Via dell'Erta Canina
San Salvatore al Monte
Convento delle Stimmatine
Via del Mte alle Croci
GALILEI
Porte Sante
Viuzzo delle Corti
San Miniato al Monte
Via delle
Cimitero delle Porte Sante
Giramonte
GALILEO
VIALE
Passo all'Erta
Via del
Viuzzo di Gattaia
G
H
J

Cappella Brancacci

TOP 25

HIGHLIGHTS

- Masaccio's *Expulsion of Adam and Eve from Paradise*
- Masaccio's *St. Peter heals the Sick*
- Filippino Lippi's *St. Paul Visits St. Peter in Prison*
- Masaccio's *Tribute Money*

Part of the thrill of the Cappella Brancacci is observing in Masaccio's frescoes the power of expression and technical brilliance that inspired the Florentine painters of the 15th century.

Miniature gem This tiny chapel is reached via the cloisters of the otherwise rather dull Santa Maria del Carmine. Two layers of frescoes commissioned in 1424 by Felice Brancacci, a wealthy Florentine merchant and statesman, illustrate the life of St. Peter, shown in his orange gown. The frescoes were designed by Masolino da Panicale, who began painting them with his brilliant pupil, Masaccio. In 1428 Masaccio took over from Masolino but died that year, aged 27; the rest of the frescoes were completed in the 1480s by Filippino Lippi.

From left: Masolino's Temptation of Adam and Eve *(1425–27) is medieval in style, with an almost expressionless Adam and Eve; contrast it with the emerging Renaissance style of Masaccio's* Expulsion of Adam and Eve *(left),* The Tribute Money *(middle top) and* Raising of the Son of Theophilus and St. Peter Enthroned *(middle bottom)*

Restoration revelations In the 1980s the chapel was restored, with the removal of accumulated candle soot and layers of an 18th-century egg-based gum (which had formed a mould). The frescoes now have an intense radiance that makes it possible to see very clearly the shifts in emphasis between Masolino's work and that of Masaccio; contrast the serenity of Masolino's *Temptation of Adam and Eve,* with its soft colours and graceful figures, with the grief-stricken pair in Masaccio's *Expulsion of Adam and Eve from Paradise*. The restoration also highlighted Masaccio's mastery of chiaroscuro (light and shade), which, together with his grasp of perspective and ability to create amazingly life-like figures, set him apart from his contemporaries, many of whom deliberately copied his style.

THE BASICS

museicivicifiorentini.comune.fi.it

D6

Santa Maria del Carmine, Piazza del Carmine (enter through the cloisters)

055 276 8558; 055 276 8224 (advance reservations mandatory)

Mon, Wed–Sat 10–5, Sun 1–5. Entrance by reservation only

6, D

Poor

Moderate

Giardino di Boboli

Sculptures are dotted throughout the Boboli Gardens and the Isolotto

THE BASICS

uffizi.it
E8
Piazza Pitti
055 238 8786
Jun–Aug daily 8.15–7.30; Apr–May, Sep daily 8.15–6.30; Mar, Oct daily 8.15–5.30; Nov–Feb daily 8.15–4.30; closed 1st and last Mon of month
D
Good; some steps
Expensive, includes Gardens, Museo delle Porcellane, Galleria del Costume (both ▷ 86) and Museo degli Argenti (▷ 85)

HIGHLIGHTS

- Bacchus fountain (1560)
- La Grotta Grande, a Mannerist cave-cum-sculpture gallery (1583–88)
- Views of the hills from the Giardino dei Cavallieri
- Limonaia (1785)—protected trees from the frost; now a huge garden shed
- The Isolotto

The Boboli Gardens are, quite literally, a breath of fresh air. They are the only easily accessible reservoir of greenery in central Florence, and a lovely retreat after a hard day's sightseeing.

Renaissance origins The Boboli Gardens were created for the Medici when they moved to the Palazzo Pitti in 1550. They represent a superb example of Italian Renaissance gardening, an interplay between nature and artifice expressed in a geometric arrangement of fountains, grass and low box hedges. In 1766 they were opened to the public, and in 1992 an entrance charge was imposed.

Amphitheatre Just behind the Palazzo Pitti is the amphitheatre, built where the stone for the palazzo was quarried. It was the site of the first-ever opera performance and is surrounded by mazelike alleys of fragrant, dusty bay trees. Go uphill past the Neptune Fountain (1565–68) to reach the Giardino dei Cavallieri, where roses and peonies wilt in the summer sun. The pretty building nearby houses the Museo delle Porcellane (Porcelain Museum, ▷ 86).

More to see The Viottolone, an avenue of cypresses planted in 1637 and studded with classical statues, leads to the Isolotto, an island set in a murky green pond dotted with crumbling statues. In the middle is a copy of Giambologna's *Oceanus* fountain (1576), the original of which is in the Bargello (▷ 24–25).

The Four Evangelists on the sacristy ceiling (left); Romanesque facade (right)

TOP 25 San Miniato al Monte

Standing on a hill to the south of Florence, San Miniato is a wonderful sight, its marble facade glistening in the sunlight. Close up it is even more appealing—a jewel of the Romanesque.

Christian martyr San Miniato (St. Minias) came to Florence from the Levant in the third century and was martyred in the Roman amphitheatre that stood on the site of Piazza della Signoria, by order of the Emperor Decius. It is said that his decapitated body picked up his head and walked into the hills. His shrine, the site of the present church, was built where he finally collapsed. The church was initially run by Benedictine monks, then by Cluniacs, and finally, from 1373 to now, by the Olivetans. In the Benedictine shop, on the right as you exit, monks sell honey and herbal potions.

An eagle visitation The church was built in 1018, with a green-and-white marble facade added at the end of the 11th century and mosaics in the 13th. On the pinnacle a gilded copper statue of an eagle carries a bale of cloth: This is the symbol of the Arte di Calimala, the wool importers' guild, which supported the church in the Middle Ages.

Miraculous crucifix Inside, an inlaid floor (*c.*1207) incorporates zodiac and animal themes. In the nave is a chapel (1448) by Michelozzo, built to house a miraculous crucifix that is now in Santa Trìnita.

THE BASICS

sanminiatoalmonte.it
H9
Via Monte alle Croce, off Viale Galileo Galilei
055 234 2731
Mon–Sat 9.30–1, 3–7, Sun 8.15–7
12, 13
Poor (make inquiries)
Free

HIGHLIGHTS

- Marble facade
- Inlaid floor
- Mosaics in the apse
- Cappella del Crocifisso
- Wooden ceiling
- Cardinal of Portugal Chapel (1473)

Palazzo Pitti

TOP 25

HIGHLIGHTS

- Frescoed ceilings by Pietro da Cortona, Galleria Palatina
- Raphael's *Madonna of the Chair* (c.1516)
- Titian's overtly sexual *Mary Magdalene* (c.1531)
- Van Dyck's *Charles I and Henrietta Maria* (c.1632)
- Titian's *Portrait of a Gentleman* (1540)

TIPS

- It makes sense to concentrate on the Galleria Palatina before moving on to another gallery.
- Be prepared for crowds, and sections to be closed.
- Book ahead.
- Leave time to relax afterwards in the Giardino di Boboli (▷ 82). Combined tickets can be bought.

The Pitti Palace, with its eight museums and galleries, is unremittingly opulent, an architectural complex celebrating the power and wealth of the Medici, Florence's ruling family.

The building The wealthy banker Luca Pitti, a business rival of the Medici, commissioned architect Filippo Brunelleschi to design a vast palazzo for his family in 1457. A century later, the Pitti coffers were empty and the palace, ironically, was purchased by Eleonora de' Medici; her family filled the palace with their art collections over the next few centuries.

The paintings The Galleria Palatina houses the picture collection, comprising works just as important as those in the Uffizi and still hung in

Clockwise from left: Cortona's ceiling fresco in the Sala di Marte inside the Palatine Gallery depicts the Roman God of War; the home of the Medici family for three centuries, the imposing Palazzo Pitti was designed in 1458 and enlarged in the 16th century; the vast piazza outside the main entrance

tightly filled tiers, as they would have been in the 18th century. Masterpieces hang casually side by side with less important works, and some paintings are difficult to see. Amidst the jumble, you'll find major works by Filippo Lippi and Raphael, two superb paintings by Titian and a dramatic Caravaggio.

Other collections The Galleria leads to the stunningly extravagant and beautifully restored Appartamenti Reali (State Rooms), a chain of interconnecting rooms running along one side of the palazzo. These are followed by the Museo degli Argenti (Silver Museum), with a collection of luxury items that are often a triumph of wealth over good taste. Elsewhere, you'll find the Galleria del Costume (▷ 86) and the Galleria d'Arte Moderna (▷ 86).

THE BASICS

polomuseale.firenze.it
E7
Piazza Pitti
Galleria Palatina 055 238 8614; reservations 055 294 833
Galleria Palatina Tue–Sun 8.15–6.50; closed Jan. Argenti (▷ 82; same as Giardino di Boboli)
D
Good
Galleria Palatina, Royal Apartments expensive; Galleria d'Arte Moderna combined ticket expensive; Museo degli Argenti (▷ 82, Boboli Gardens)

More to See

FORTE DI BELVEDERE

museicivicifiorentini.comune.fi.it

This imposing fortress was built by the Medici in 1590 as a refuge for the Grand Dukes in their struggle against the Florentine Republic, and a reminder of Medici military might.

F8 Via San Leonardo 055 262 5962 View from the road D, plus walk Free

GALLERIA D'ARTE MODERNA

uffizi.it

More than 30 rooms of paintings here span the mid-18th to mid-20th centuries. It is located in the main building of the Palazzo Pitti on the floor above the Palatina.

E7 Palazzo Pitti, Piazza Pitti 055 238 8616 Tue–Sun 8.15–6.50 D Good Inclusive ticket with Galleria Palatina (▷ 84) expensive

GALLERIA DEL COSTUME

uffizi.it

In the Palazzina Meridiana in the south wing of the Pitti, this is one for devotees of clothes and fashion. The collection illustrates the history of costume from the 18th century up until the 1920s.

E7 Palazzo Pitti, Piazza Pitti 055 238 8713 Giardino di Boboli (▷ 82, panel) D Good Inclusive ticket with Museo degli Argenti, Museo delle Porcellane, Giardino di Boboli expensive

MUSEO DELLE PORCELLANE

uffizi.it

French, Italian, German and Viennese porcelain and ceramics are all housed in a pavilion at the top of the Giardino di Boboli.

E8 Giardino di Boboli, Piazza Pitti 055 238 8709 Giardino di Boboli (▷ 82, panel) D Good, some steps Inclusive ticket with Museo degli Argenti, Galleria del Costume and Giardino di Boboli expensive

MUSEO DELLA SPECOLA

"La Specola" is so called after the observatory that used to be here. This museum of zoology and natural history is part of the university. An unusual highlight is the Cere

View from Piazzale Michelangelo

Anatomiche, a gruesome set of 18th-century wax models of bits of human bodies.
E7 Via Romana 17 055 228 8251 Jun–Sep Tue–Sun 10.30–5.30; Oct–May Tue–Sun 9.30–4.30 11, D Good Expensive

PIAZZALE MICHELANGELO

Despite the fact that Piazzale Michelangelo is frequented by busloads of tourists, this stupendous vantage point is still very much worth the trip. Ignore the poor green copy of Michelangelo's *David* and crop of souvenir stalls, beware of pickpockets and soak up the wonderful view.
H8 Viale Galileo Galilei 12, 13 Good Free

PONTE ALLE GRAZIE

Dating from 1237, when it was known as Ponte Rubaconte (after the chief magistrate who commissioned it), the bridge was rebuilt to its 18th-century design after World War II. Its present name is from the oratory of Santa Maria delle Grazie, which once stood here.
G7 C3, D, 6

SANTA FELICITA

This second-century church is the second-oldest in Florence, after San Lorenzo. The highlight is Pontormo's Mannerist *Deposition* (1525–28) in the Cappella Caponi: a stunning vortex of contorted forms in vibrant shades of pink, blue and green.
F7 Piazza Santa Felicita 055 213 018 Mon–Sat 9–12, 3.30–5.30; closed during services. Mass: Sun 9, 11, Mon–Sat 6pm D Poor Free

SANTO SPIRITO

basilicasantospirito.it

Designed by Filippo Brunelleschi in 1435, this church has an unfinished 18th-century baroque facade. The *cenacolo* (refectory) houses a fresco of the *Last Supper* by Nardo di Cione.
E7 Piazza Santo Spirito 055 210 030 Thu–Tue 10–12.30, 4–5.30; closed during services D Poor Free

Santo Spirito

Around the Oltrarno

This walk begins amid the bustle of the Oltrarno, yet soon passes through more tranquil surroundings to catch a glimpse of local life.

DISTANCE: 2km (1 mile) **ALLOW:** 2–3 hours

START

PONTE VECCHIO (▷ 34–35)
F7 C3

❶ In summer this walk can be baking hot; start early in the morning or after 4pm and take a bottle of water. Plan a midday picnic at the Forte di Belvedere (▷ 86).

❷ Set off from the south side of the Ponte Vecchio in Oltrarno. With your back to the bridge, take the first square on your left, Piazza di Santa Felicita.

❸ Here you will find Pontormo's *Deposition* in Santa Felicita (▷ 87) church. Take the road on the left of the church, the Costa di San Giorgio, where Galileo lived at No. 19.

❹ Continue up its steep slope. At the top, you pass through Porta di San Giorgio (1260), the oldest city gate, with a carving of St. George slaying the dragon.

❺ Follow Via del Belvedere, and leave the 1590 Forte di Belvedere on your right.

❻ After the entrance to Fort di Belvedere, descend steeply along the 13th-century defensive city walls. At the bottom of the hill, by the small gateway of Porta San Miniato, turn right and head up Via del Monte alle Croci.

❼ A little way up take the steep Via di San Salvadore al Monte on the left, which crosses Viale Galileo Galilei. Climb the hill flanked by cypress trees that continues up toward San Miniato (▷ 83). Return to Viale Galileo Galilei and go right.

❽ Continue downhill to Piazzale Michelangelo for great views. A No. 12 bus will take you back down to Ponte alle Grazie (▷ 87).

END

PIAZZALE MICHELANGELO (▷ 87)
H8 12, 13

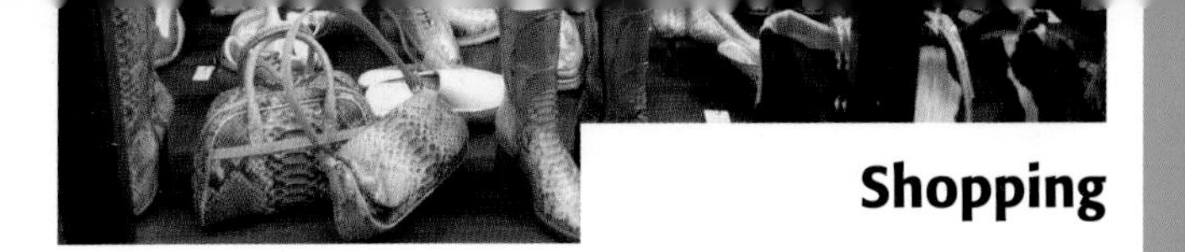

Shopping

ANNA

annapitti.it

This shop is in a 300-year-old tower in front of the Pitti Palace. Anna sells a great range of leather goods, knitwear, scarves and ties for men and women.

E7 Piazza Pitti 38–40r 055 283 787 D

ANTICO SETIFICIO FIORENTINO

anticosetificiofiorentino.it

Only if you fix up an appointment in advance can you visit this old Florentine silk factory that provides fabric for some of Italy's most sought-after designers. Much of the fabric is woven using traditional methods and 18th-century looms.

C6 Via Lorenzo Bartolini 4 055 213 861 D

BARTOLOZZI & MAIOLI

This antiques shop gives an insight into the Florentine love of ostentatious adornment. As you wander you can hear craftsmen tapping. The quality is excellent but pieces are expensive.

E7 Via Vellutini 5r 055 281 723 D

BOTTEGA DELLE STAMPE

bottegadellestampe.com

Framed and unframed antique or art nouveau prints (known in Italy as Liberty) are on sale in this elegant store.

E6 Borgo San Jacopo 56r 055 295 396 D

LA CASA DELLA STAMPA

Vivianna is the lithographer who hand-tints many of these beautiful prints. There is a huge selection of Florentine scenes, from the Medici era and painted studies of butterflies and plants.

E7 Sdrucciolo de Pitti 11r 055 285 755 D

ENOTECA PERI

A no-nonsense wine and oil shop selling good-quality regional products, this enoteca lies just over the Santa Trìnita bridge.

E7 Via Maggio 5r 055 212 674 D

FARMACIA PITTI

It's worth walking through this former 15th-century herbalist shop just to see the sales room at the back decked out with antique glass jars and old cabinets, but there's a modern working pharmacy here too.

E7 Piazza San Felice 4r 055 224 402 D, 6

GIULIO GIANNINI E FIGLIO

giuliogiannini.it

The best known of Florence's stationery shops, established in 1856, sells tasteful cards and books bound in leather, as well as beautifully finished desktop paraphernalia, letter racks and pen holders, all covered with marbled paper.

E7 Piazza Pitti 37r 055 212 621 D

POTTERY FACTS

Traditional Italian ceramics are known as majolica, terracotta covered with a brilliant tin-based glaze. Arabic ceramics inspired pots made for the Medici court at Montelupo, to the west of Florence. Deruta in Umbria makes flowery designs in blue on white or yellow. Designs in turquoise on white are also much in evidence. Tuscan peasant wares, white or yellow, splashed with green or blue spots, are increasingly popular. Among the best-known classic designs is Gran Faenza, with green, red and blue floral designs on a pale grey-blue background. Most shops offer shipping.

J. T. CASINI

jennifertattanelli.it

The latest in Italian and international designer clothing for women is on sale here. Up-and-coming designers are showcased alongside well-known brands.

E7 · Piazza Pitti 30–31r · 055 219 324 · D

MADOVA GLOVES

madova.com

This family-run business, with its factory at the back of the shop, was established in 1919 and sells fine gloves lined with silk, cashmere and fur in every hue.

E7 · Via Guicciardini 1r · 055 239 6526 · D

MOLERIA LOCCHI

locchi.com

This shop, deep in the southern reaches of the Oltrarno, sells the most extraordinary glass you will see outside Venice, created using traditional methods.

C7 · Via Domenico Burchiello 10 · 055 229 8371 · D, 12, 13

OLIO & CONVIVIUM

oliorestaurant.it

This pristine delicatessen has beautiful displays of bakery goods, cheeses, charcuterie and a huge range of olive oils and wine. There's an adjoining restaurant.

E6 · Via Santo Spirito 4 · 055 265 8198 · D, 11

RIVE GAUCHE

rivegaucheshoes.com

Many people visit Florence to buy the leather goods for which the city is renowned, in particular shoes. This shop takes you back in time with its beautiful handmade shoes and boots.

E7 · Via Guicciardini 31r · 055 213 474 · D

ARTISANS

The district of Oltrarno is characterized by small artisan workshops producing leather goods, textiles, ceramics, paper products and jewellery. Many of these businesses have been in the same family for generations and extreme skill and passion is employed in the workmanship.

SFORNO

ilsantobevitore.com

Rather than the usual Italian-style goods, Sforno makes mouthwatering brownies, cheesecake, frangipane tarts, savoury quiches and a whole range of different pizzas by the slice. At lunchtime there are also salads and soups to eat in or take away.

D7 · Via Santa Monaca 3r · 055 239 8580 · C3, D

STEFANO BEMER

stefanobemer.it

For exquisitely made men's shoes, head to this ex-chapel in San Niccolò, where you'll find Oxfords, Derbys, monkstraps, moccasins—bespoke or ready to wear—plus elegant belts, wallets and watch straps. Prices are high but the shoes will last a lifetime.

H7 · Via San Niccolò 2 · 055 060 476 · C3, D

IL TORCHIO

legatoriailtorchio.com

As you walk into this stationery shop you are instantly aware that this is a place where things are made, not just a showroom. You can buy sheets of marbled paper or have it made up to suit your requirements. There are also ready-made marbled paper goods available.

F7 · Via dei Bardi 17 · 055 234 2862 · C, D

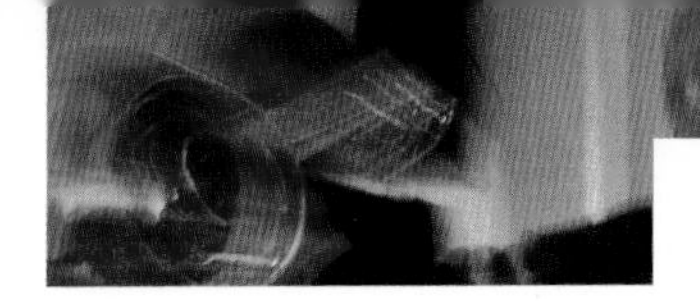

Entertainment and Nightlife

LA DOLCE VITA

dolcevitaflorence.com

This is one of the hippest places for young Florentines to hang out and mingle with the pre-club *bella gente*. It stays open until 2am.

D6 Piazza del Carmine 6r 055 284 595 D, 6

HEMINGWAY

hemingwayfirenze.com

A chic, funky café/bar just off Piazza del Carmine, Hemingway serves light meals, great cocktails, speciality teas, fine coffees and chocolates, and stays open late.

D6 Piazza Piattellina 9r 055 284 781 D, 6

UNIVERSALE

universalefirenze.it

This former cinema space is now dedicated to dance music, cocktail drinking and Italian food. The music is house during the week and more eclectic on Saturday, with funk, jazz and exotica.

C6 Via Pisana 77r 055 221 122 Closed Mon, Tue, Wed 6, 12

DRINKING LAWS

The legal age for buying alcohol in bars or shops is 18. Opening times for licensed premises are not set, although there are restrictions before, during and after some football (soccer) matches. Laws against drinking and driving are firmly enforced.

VOLUME

volume.it

This popular retro-chic Oltrarno haunt on lovely Piazza Santo Spirito is open all day, but things really get lively at aperitivo time, when the music cranks up and punters spill onto the terrace.

E7 Piazza Santo Spirito 5r 055 238 1460 C3, D, 6, 11

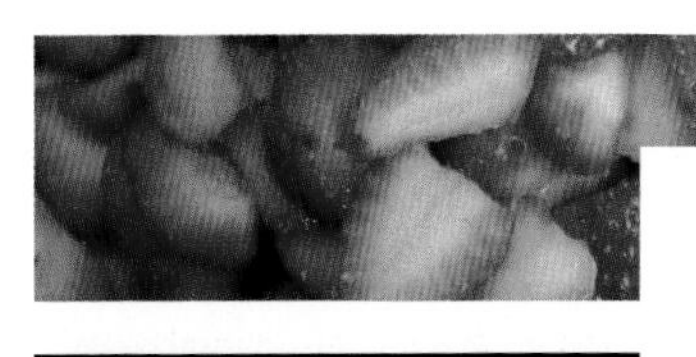

Where to Eat

PRICES

Prices are approximate, based on a 3-course meal for one person.

€€€ over €55
€€ €35–€55
€ under €35

AL TRANVAI (€)

altranvai.it

Diners pack into this lively trattoria on a quiet neighbourhood square in the Oltrarno. Popular (with locals) is *frattaglie* (a mind-boggling range of offal) but the menu changes every day.

C7 Piazza Torquato Tasso 14r 055 225 197 Tue–Sat 12.15–3, 7–10.45, Mon 7–10.45 12, 13

BURRO E ACCIUGHE (€€)

burroeacciughe.com

Butter and Anchovies is a retro-rustic restaurant specializing in fish and seafood dishes. Expect marinated salmon, tagliatelle with sea bream and rocket and olive pesto, and grilled tuna steak, plus a good selection of wines.

C6 Via dell'Orto 35r 055 045 7286 Tue–Thu 7–midnight, Fri–Sun 12–2, 7–midnight D, 6

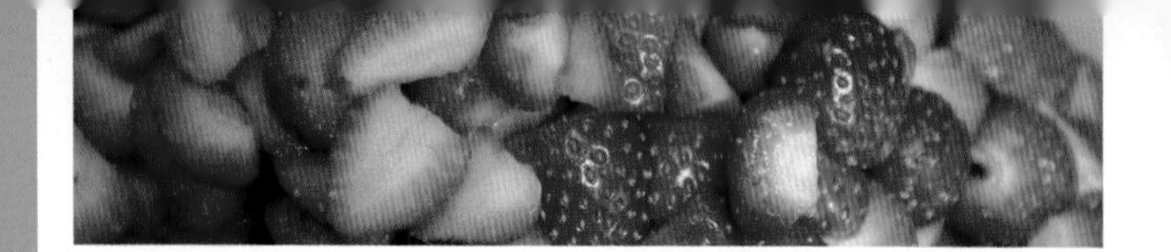

CAMMILLO (€€–€€€)

The Masiero family's long-established trattoria attracts a fashionable crowd and Italian celebrities, enticed by the home-made pasta, *baccalà* (salted cod) dishes and expertly cooked meats. Try some of the house virgin olive oil with bread.

E6 Borgo San Jacopo 57r 055 212 427 Thu–Mon 12–2.30, 7.30–10.30 D

LA CASALINGA (€–€€)

trattorialacasalinga.it

A busy and down-to-earth family-run trattoria serving rustic Florentine fare, this is a good place to try *bollito* (boiled meat) and *ribollita*, the Florentine soup made with bread and vegetables.

B8 Via dei Michelozzi 9r 055 218 624 Mon–Sat 12–2.30, 7–10 D

DEL CARMINE (€–€€)

With its pleasant terrace and menu of daily specials, this traditional neighbourhood trattoria is popular with Oltrarno locals and visitors. Try the *tagliata*—sliced grilled steak topped with rocket and parmesan shavings.

D6 Piazza del Carmine 18r 055 218 601 Mon–Sat 12.15–2.30, 7.15–10.30 C3, D, 6

CONTRADICTION

The concept of vegetarianism is not one that sits easily with Italian ideas about food, and there are very few vegetarian restaurants in Italy. However, there are few better countries for those who do not eat meat (or fish). Many pasta dishes contain no meat—pesto, tomato sauce or ravioli stuffed with spinach and ricotta, to name but a few. For a main course, try *grigliata di verdura* (grilled vegetables) or restaurant staples such as *parmigiana di melanzane* (aubergine layered with tomato and mozzarella, and baked with a Parmesan crust), *mozzarella in carrozza* (fried mozzarella) and *frittate* (omelettes).

OLIVIA (€)

oliviafirenze.com

To taste Tuscany's "liquid gold" (extra virgin olive oil), try this bright little shop-cum-restaurant that sells all things olive oil related. Everything on the menu is prepared with lashings of extra virgin, even the ice cream.

E7 Piazza Pitti 14r 055 267 0359 Tue–Sun 11.30–5.30 C3, D

IL SANTO BEVITORE (€€)

ilsantobevitore.com

Offering a creative take on Tuscan and Italian classics, Santo Bevitore has long been one of Florence's most fashionable restaurants. The menu is based around fresh, seasonal ingredients.

D6 Via Santo Spirito 64–66r 055 211 264 Mon 7.30–11, Tue–Sun 12.30–2.30, 7.30–11 C3, D, 6, 11

SANTO SPIRITO (€–€€)

osteriasantospirito.it

This charming trattoria has outdoor seating and a menu of robust main courses such as oven-baked gnocchi in cheese and flavoured with truffles. It's good for vegetarians and great for kids.

E7 Piazza Santo Spirito 16r 055 238 2383 Daily 11–11 D, 11

LE VOLPI E L'UVA (€)

levolpieluva.com

The Foxes and Grapes is a delightful little wine bar tucked away behind the Ponte Vecchio where you can wash down pungent Italian salamis and cheeses with wines from all over Italy.

F7 Piazza dei Rossi 1r 055 239 8132 Mon–Sat 11–9 C3, D

There is plenty to do to escape the crowds or to have a change of scenery. Choose from pretty Fiesole, only 7km (4 miles) away; try medieval Siena and Lucca, or the Leaning Tower of Pisa, providing an irresistible pull.

IL SODO
VIA DELLE PANCHE
CAREGGI
LIPPI
TRE PIETRE
LE PANCHE
LA PIETRA
VIA BOLOGNESE
VIALE ALESSANDRO GUIDONI
PONTE DI MEZZO
IL POGGETTO
Museo Stibbert
Giardino San Donato
VIA FRANCESCO BARACCA
VIA VITTORIO EMANUELE II
IL PELLEGRINO
VIA CIRCONDARIA
IL ROMITO
VIALE FRANCESCO REDI
VIA MARAGLIANO
Giardino dell' Orticoltura
Torrente Mugnone
SAN JACOPINO
VIA DEL PONTE ALLE MOSSE
VIALE GIACOMO MATTEOTTI
Fortezza da Basso
Le Cascine
V FILIPPO STROZZI
VIA CAVOUR
Giardino dei Semplici
VIA VALFONDA
VIA GUELFA
Giardino della Gherardesca
VIALE FRATELLI ROSSELLI
V LUIGI ALAMANNI
VIA DELLA SCALA
VIALE ABRAMO LINCOLN
SAN GIOVANNI
SANTA MARIA NOVELLA
BORGO PINTI
Arno
L AMERIGO VESPUCCI
PIGNONE
VIA PISANA
VIA D FONDERIA
VIA DE FOSSI
MONTICELLI
L SODERINI
SAN FREDIANO
FIRENZE
SANTA CROCE
VIALE ALEARDO ALEARDI
L GEN DIAZ
SANTO SPIRITO
L DELLE GRAZIE
Giardino Torrigiani
VIA DE SERRAGLI
VIALE FRANCESCO PETRARCA
L SERRISTORI
OLIVUZZO
SAN NICCOLÒ
Giardino di Boboli
BELLOSGUARDO
BOBOLINO
VIALE GALILEO
Cimitero delle Porte Sante
VIA SENESE
VIA DEL POGGIO IMPERIALE
GAMBERAIA
SAN GAGGIO
MARIGNOLLE
LE DUE STRADE
POGGIO IMPERIALE
Certosa del Galluzzo

VIA BOLOGNESE
BORGUNTO
Fiesole
PONTE ALLA BADIA
410
Monte Ceceri
CAMERATA
LAPO
MAIANO
VIALE SAN DOMENICO
LE CURE
VIALE AUGUSTO RIGHI
SAN GERVASIO
VIALE DEI MILLE
VIA DELLE CENTO STELLE
VIALE MANFREDO FANTI
COVERCIANO
CAMPO DI MARTE
PONTE A MENSOLA
VIA DEGLI ARTISTI
V. ANTONIO GRAMSCI
VIALE EDMONDO DE AMICIS
VIA LUNGO L'AFFRICO
VIA DEL GIGNORO
SAN SALVI
VIA VINCENZO GIOBERTI
VIA ARETINA
MADONNONE
VIALE GIOVINE ITALIA
VIA PIAGENTINA
BELLARIVA
VARLUNGO
Arno
L DEL TEMPIO
L CRISTOFORO COLOMBO
L FRANCESCO FERRUCCI
VIA DI VILLAMAGNA
VIA COLUCCIO SALUTATI
RICORBOLI
LE LAME
GAVINANA
NAVE A ROVEZZANO
VIALE MICHELANGIOLO
VIALE EUROPA
BANDINO
VIA MARCO POLO
SORGANE
SAN MARCELLINO
VIA GIOVANNI AGNELLI
0
1 km
0
½ mile

Typical Tuscan countryside (left); Fiesole's amphitheatre (below) and bell tower (right)

TOP 25

Fiesole

Perched on a hillside 7km (4 miles) above Florence, this delightful Etruscan-Roman town offers outstanding views over the city and the chance to visit an impressive archaeological complex, complete with amphitheatre, baths and a temple.

Take a stroll Fiesole is the perfect antidote to hectic sightseeing in central Florence, while the bus ride there, climbing the winding road, is a pleasing introduction to the Tuscan countryside. Head first to the tourist information office to pick up a town map, which includes three walking routes that take in the best views.

The archaeological area The entrance ticket to Fiesole's important Roman and Etruscan remains includes the Museo Civico and the small Museo Bandini. Set high up on a hillside, the open-air site features an Etruscan temple, the superbly preserved first-century AD Roman amphitheatre and the partially restored Roman baths. The theatre, holding 3,000 people, is still used today for performances and concerts during the Fiesole Summer Festival (▷ 103). On Via Dupré, Museo Bandini houses 13th- to 15th-century Florentine paintings and Luca della Robbia terracottas.

Around the town Landmarks include the Duomo, with its 13th-century bell tower, and the striking 14th-century Palazzo Communale, now occupied by the town council. Traditional restaurants and cafés overlook the main square.

THE BASICS

museidifiesole.it

See map ▷ 95

Via Portigiani 3–5

055 596 1239

Archaeological area and museum Apr–Sep, Nov–Feb Wed–Mon 10–3; Mar, Oct Wed–Mon 10–6. Museo Bandini Apr–Sep Fri–Sun 9–7; Mar, Oct Fri–Sun 10–6; Nov–Feb Fri–Sun 9–3

7

Good

Combined ticket expensive

HIGHLIGHTS

- Views over Florence
- Archaeological area
- Roman amphitheatre
- Walks in the Tuscan countryside

More to See

LE CASCINE

Once the site of the Medici dairy farms (*cascine*), Florence's largest park is a 20- to 30-minute walk west of the city centre. It has an open-air swimming pool and a market every Tuesday. The area can be rather seedy by night.

A3 Ponte della Vittoria Daily 24 hours 17, 18 Good Free

CERTOSA DEL GALLUZZO

cistercensi.info/certosadifirenze

This great Carthusian monastery was once occupied by 18 monks, who lived silent lives. The stunning Chiostro Grande is decorated with *tondi* (circular works of art) by Andrea and Giovanni della Robbia. The visit includes the Palazzo degli Studi, which holds the *Scenes from the Passion* frescoes executed by Pontormo while he was sheltered here during the 1522 plague.

See map ▷ 94 Certosa del Galluzzo, Via Buca di Certosa 2 055 204 9226 Tue–Sat 9.15–11.15, 3–5 37 Good Free or donation Guided tours only

FORTEZZA DA BASSO

An enormous defensive fortress built in 1534 by Antonio da Sangallo il Giovane to the orders of Alessandro de' Medici, this citadel now hosts trade fairs, exhibitions and other events while cars and buses hurtle past on all sides.

E3 Viale Filippo Strozzi Contact tourist office for events 4, 12, 13, 14, 20, 23

MUSEO STIBBERT

museostibbert.it

This bizarre museum, with its superb armour collection, makes a fascinating diversion. The collection was amassed by Frederick Stibbert (1838–1906), who travelled the world, purchasing armour, porcelain, paintings, costumes and much more. The museum is set in pleasant wooded grounds, complete with an Egyptian-style folly.

See map ▷ 94 Via Frederico Stibbert 26 055 486 049 Mon–Wed 10–2, Fri–Sun 10–6 4 to Via Vittorio Emanuele II and steep walk to museum Access to most parts Moderate Café, bookshop

Altar in the 14th-century Certosa del Galluzzo

Excursions

LUCCA

The historic centre of this prosperous town is entirely enclosed within intact Renaissance walls, inside which lies a rich heritage of churches and palaces. The best starting point for a tour of the town is Piazza Napoleone, with all the main sights only a few minutes' walk away. Begin at the Duomo, and its Museo della Cattedrale, then cross the square to Santi Giovanni e Reparata. Via Fillungo is an expensive shopping street that leads north to the Piazza Anfiteatro (which retains the shape of the amphitheatre it is named after) and San Frediano, another outstanding church. The main museums lie inside the walls to the west and east of the heart of town. Walking around the 4km-long (2.5-mile) walls gives a fine overview of the town and spectacular views of the countryside farther afield—all the way to the Apuan Alps, which are covered in snow in winter.

THE BASICS

luccaturismo.it
Distance: 50km (31 miles)
Journey Time: About 1 hour
Regular departures from Santa Maria Novella station to Lucca Centrale
Piazza Santa Maria 35, Porto San Donato, Pizzzale Verdi
0583 962 233

PISA

The main draw is the architecture of the Campo dei Miracoli (Field of Miracles), home to the famous Leaning Tower, reopened in 2001 after years of work to steady the tilt. Make sure you buy tickets in advance if you want to climb it, as numbers are severely restricted. The tower stands next to the Romanesque-Gothic Duomo and Baptistery, the largest in Italy. All three buildings date from the 11th and 12th centuries, at the height of Pisa's power. There is, however, much more to Pisa than just its tower. The city is home to some 87,500 residents and there are more than 20 churches, many impressive palazzi and several historic bridges to be explored. The pleasant cobbled streets of the shopping centre are a good place to stroll and find a café or restaurant. Check out the markets and mingle with the locals away from the tourist area around the tower. The daily food market (7–1.30) held in Piazza delle Vettovaglie, just off Borgo Stretto, is particularly lively.

THE BASICS

pisaunicaterra.it
Distance: 80km (50 miles)
Journey Time: 1 hour
Regular departures from Santa Maria Novella station to Pisa Centrale Station
Piazza Vittorio Emanuele II 16 (outside station)
050 422 91

THE BASICS

terresiena.it
enjoysiena.it
Distance: 66km (41 miles)
Journey Time: 1–2 hours
Regular departures from Santa Maria Novella station
Rapide Sita bus leaves the Florence bus station for Piazza San Domenico in Siena
Piazza del Campo 56
0577 280 551

SIENA

One of the loveliest towns in Italy, Siena has magnificent museums, a superb Duomo, good restaurants and interesting shops. The focal point is fan-shaped Piazza del Campo, which slopes down to the Palazzo Pubblico with its skinny bell tower. The Gothic cathedral was built between 1136 and 1382. Outside is a vast unfinished nave, begun in 1339 with the intention of making this the world's largest cathedral. Work was abandoned during the plague of 1348. Siena is home to the famous Palio, a horse race held in Piazza del Campo on 2 July and 16 August. Tickets for the event sell out months in advance; it is possible to stand but it does get very crowded and can be very hot. For a sense of Siena's size and layout, get a bird's-eye view by climbing the Torre del Mangia or the old cathedral wall. The historic centre of the city is closed to traffic, making it easy for pedestrians, and fortunately all the main sights are in close proximity and easily walkable.

THE BASICS

sangimignano.com
Distance: 57km (35 miles)
Journey Time: 1 hour
Route: Take the Firenze/Siena *raccordo* (a motorway link road) until the Poggibonsi exit. Follow the signs from here to San Gimignano—around 6km (4 miles)
Museo Leonardiano
Castello dei Conti Guidi, Vinci
0571 933 251
Mar–Oct daily 9.30–7; Nov–Feb daily 9.30–6; museoleonardiano.it
Moderate

TUSCAN COUNTRYSIDE

Much-visited San Gimignano is a prime destination with its hilltop site and famous medieval towers. It is the archetypical Tuscan town, perched on a hilltop and surrounded by vineyards, olive groves and cypress trees. The towers of the medieval town can be seen from some distance away. Only 15 of the original 72 towers—built by the town's patrician residents as symbols of their wealth and power—remain, but their impact is still breathtaking. There are several museums to visit and particular products to buy, including San Gimignano white wine (Vernaccia), saffron and olive oil. For pots, stop in Montelupo, where many of Florence's ceramics have been made for centuries. On your way back visit Vinci, the birthplace of Leonardo da Vinci, with a museum about his life. If you want a swim, the village of Sambuca, near Tavarnelle, has an outdoor pool.

Shopping

Lucca

CANIPAROLI

This shop is a chocoholic's heaven. Chunks of chocolate adorn the window, along with calorific but divine cakes, such as the naughty but delicious Sachertorte.

✉ Via Paolino 96 ☎ 0583 534 56

CERAMISTI D'ARTÉ

ceramistidarte.it

Tuscan artists Stefano Seardo and Fabrizio Falchi sculpt and paint at this workshop. Pick up hand-painted decorative tiles, terracotta sculptures and marble mosaics. Everything is produced according to ancient Italian ceramic techniques.

✉ Via Santa Gemma Galgani 1 ☎ 0583 467 224

ENOTECA MARSILI

enotecamarsili.it

Marsili offers a tasty introduction to Lucca's vineyards, with some lesser-known but delicious wines. Also try some of the herb liqueurs and *digestifs* that are produced using local recipes.

✉ Piazza San Michele 38 ☎ 0583 491 751

MERCATO DEL CARMINE

Lucca's produce market is held every day except Sunday in an arched and colonnaded building. You'll find the best seasonal fruit and vegetables, deli stalls offering cheeses, cured meats and breads and a pleasant café for refreshments between shopping.

✉ Piazza del Carmine 🕑 Mon–Sat 7–1, 4–7.30

TADDEUCCI

buccellatotaddeucci.com

This shop, founded by Jacopo Taddeucci in 1881, is in Lucca's main square. It is renowned for the *buccellato*, a sweet ring-shaped cake made with raisins and flavoured with anise. There are also plenty of other tempting cakes and patisserie to choose from, together with sweets and chocolates.

✉ Piazza San Michele 34 ☎ 0583 494 933

Pisa

BACCHUS ENOTECA

bacchusenoteca.com

Just a short distance from the main train station, this specialist wine shop is the perfect place to buy Tuscan wines. You will also find spirits and liqueurs, as well as sweets, oils and other gastronomic delicacies.

✉ Via Mascagni 1 ☎ 050 500 560

FEDERICO SALZA

The Pisa outlet of the popular Turin confectioner sells beautifully fashioned chocolates and pastries. Look for the chocolate Leaning Tower of Pisa.

✉ Borgo Stretto 46 ☎ 050 580 144

SCARLATTI 1896

scarlatti1896.it

Officially a tobacconist but also a brilliant place to buy old-fashioned men's gifts, atmospheric Scarlatti has a good selection of pipes, pure badger-hair shaving

HANDICRAFTS

Tuscany has a strong artisan tradition that continues to flourish. There is a huge range of regional handicrafts to seek out, such as olive-wood bowls and plates, alabaster ware and glassware, with many products only available in the area where they are made. Florence and the surrounding area has an abundance of small craft workshops specializing in picture frames, accessories and restored antique furniture.

brushes, cut-throat razors, penknives and unusual men's fragrances.

✉ Borgo Stretto 18 ☎ 050 573 899

Siena

ANTICHITÀ MONNA AGNESE

This is one of Siena's better antiques stores, stocking furniture and silver as well as other items. There is another, smaller shop on the opposite side of the street, which deals in antique jewellery.

✉ Via di Città 45 and 60 ☎ 0577 282 288

CERAMICHE ARTISTICHE SANTA CATERINA

Marcello Neri founded this business, which he now runs with his wife and son. They all work in the traditional Sienese style of ceramics using only black, white and *terra di Siena*, or burnt siena, glass glazes. Their designs are inspired by local architecture, especially the Duomo, and you can watch them at work.

✉ Via Mattioli 12 ☎ 0577 45 006

DROGHERIA MANGANELLI

A must for foodies, this shop is a member of the Slow Food Movement, an organization that promotes organic food, grown and cooked using traditional methods. It has been selling local produce since 1879, with an array of cured meats and fine farmhouse cheeses, as well as vinegar, wine and virgin olive oils. Try the *ricciarelli* (almond cookies), traditionally served with sweet wine.

✉ Via di Citta 71–73 ☎ 0577 280 002

MORBIDI

Morbidi is one of the best-known Sienese delicatessens, selling Tuscan salamis and the unusual *finocchiona* (salami flavoured with fennel). Be sure to try the local cheeses, such as *pecorino* or the oval-shaped *fresco di Monnalisa*, and pâtés that are great for picnics. The lunchtime buffet, served in the basement, is excellent value.

✉ Via Banchi di Sopra 75 ☎ 0577 280 268

MARKETS

There are daily food markets in provincial and regional capitals and other large towns. They generally take place in a purpose-built market hall or in a specific square or street, selling meat, groceries, fish, dairy products, fruit and vegetables. Where there's a daily food market, the weekly market will be devoted to everything else, from clothes and shoes to household goods, plants and fabrics. In Florence the most prominent markets are Mercato Centrale (▷ 68), Mercato Sant'Ambrogio (▷ 38) and Mercato Nuovo (▷ 37).

SIENA RICAMA

This embroidery and needlework shop is run by Signora Fontani, who makes all the goods herself. Drawing inspiration from medieval designs, local art, frescoes and manuscripts, the beautifully embroidered or cross-stitched items include clothing, soft furnishings, lampshades and tapestries.

✉ Via di Città 61 ☎ 0577 288 339

TRAME DI STORIA

Drop into this workshop and boutique to pick up beautiful, hand-woven accessories and fashionable garments. Designer Fioretta Bacci can often be seen sitting at a loom weaving her much sought-after scarves, shawls and items of clothing.

✉ Via San Pietro 7 ☎ 0577 282 200

Entertainment and Nightlife

AUDITORIUM FLOG

flog.it

This is probably the best known of Florence's live music venues, where music of all kinds is played; regular themed disco evenings are also on the programme.

Off map Via Mercati 24b 055 477 978 4

CANOTTIERI COMUNALI FIRENZE

canottiericomunalifirenze.it

You can try your hand at boating, rowing or canoeing at this club on the River Arno. If you want to learn how to do it properly, courses are available.

L7 Lungarno Ferrucci 2 055 681 2151 D

CIRCOLO DEL GOLF DELL'UGOLINO

golfugolino.it

Founded in 1933, this attractive 18-hole, par 72 course just to the south of Florence has hosted many famous golfing greats.

Off map Via Chiantigiana 3, Grassina (10km/6miles south on road to Siena) 055 230 1009

CLUB SPORTIVO FIRENZE

clubsportivofirenze.it

Situated in Le Cascine park (▷ 98), this club has two clay tennis courts (covered in winter) in pleasant surroundings.

A4 Viale del Visarno 10 055 332 701 Mon–Sat 3–7.30 6, 6B, 12, 17 or tram

ESTATE FIESOLANA

estatefiesolana.it

This season of music, opera and ballet is primarily held in Fiesole's open-air Teatro Romano (▷ 97), from late June to September. Reserve in advance and then head for the Fiesole hills, above the city, for an unbeatable experience.

Estate Fiesolana Off map Contact APT (tourist information), Fiesole 055 596 1323

Teatro Romano Off map Via Marini 7

GIRASOL

girasol.it

Florentines have a passion for Latin American bars. This is the best, with live and recorded Cuban, Caribbean and other Latin-American music.

D1 Via del Romito 1r 055 474 948 14

GOLF CLUB MONTELUPO

golfmontelupo.it

This 3,067-yard, par 36, 9-hole golf course lies below the Chianti Montalbano hills on the banks of the Arno. Enjoy the scenery and excellent facilities, including a pro shop, practice area and putting greens. Coaching is available.

Off map Fattoria di Fibbiana, Via Fibbiana 4, Montelupo (19km/12 miles west of Florence) 0571 541 004

NELSON MANDELA FORUM

mandelaforum.it

This medium-size venue near Campo di Marte hosts some of Italy's most

MAGGIO MUSICALE FIORENTINO

This major musical festival held in May and June includes opera and ballet as well as orchestral concerts and chamber music. It has its own orchestra and chorus. The main venue is the Opera di Firenze (▷ 74); the Teatro della Pergola (▷ 74) and the Teatro Verdi (▷ 46) are used for more intimate concerts. The main box office is at the Opera di Firenze.

celebrated rock and pop acts. Check in advance for British and US bands who may be playing here.
M4 Viale P. Paoli 3 Box office Via Alamanini 055 678 841 for tickets 3, 10

PAGANELLI

Paganelli is open six days a week for swimming; there are also courses for adults and children, which include diving and aquagym.
Off map Viale Guidoni 208, Novoli 055 416 330 Closed Tue 5, 22

PALAZZO DEI CONGRESSI

This palazzo hosts many conferences and cultural events throughout the year.
E3 Viale Filippo Strozzi Box office Via Alamanini 055 210 804 for tickets; check with tourist office for events 6, 11, 22, 36, 37, A

PINOCCHIO JAZZ

pinocchiojazz.it

Some of Italy's top jazz artists play here during the two-season agenda. Members nod approvingly in this smoky venue while musicians play into the night. Check *Firenze Spettacolo* for what's on.

FOOTBALL IS ALL

Many Florentines take more pride in their football (soccer) team than in their artistic heritage. Until 2002 AC Fiorentina, also known as the "Viola" (the Purples), were one of the top clubs in Italy, but following a financial scandal the club was declared bankrupt and demoted three divisions. The team clawed its way back into Serie A and regained its former glory. Games take place at the Stadio Artemio Franchi, where you can join the ever-faithful fans cheering on the lads in lavender.

M8 Viale Giannotti 13 055 683 388 31, 32

PISCINA COMUNALE BELLARIVA

The popular Bellariva (officially Goffredo Nannini communal pool) offers an outdoor Olympic-sized swimming pool with a smaller one for children in pleasant shady gardens east of the city. There's a restaurant on site too.
M7 Lungarno A. Moro 055 626 6007 Jun–Sep Mon–Fri 10–6, Sat–Sun 10–7 14

PISCINA LE PAVONIERE

Located within the Cascine park (▷ 98), this is the most popular—and the prettiest—outdoor swimming pool in Florence.
A4 Viale della Catena 055 362 233 Summer only, daily 10–7 17 or tram

STADIO COMUNALE ARTEMIO FRANCHI

The Stadio Comunale Artemio Franchi, or the Palazzo dello Sport, is where AC Fiorentina (▷ panel) play football on alternate Sundays from September to May. Tickets are sold at the entrance and in cafés near by.
L3 Campo di Marte, Viale Manfredo Fanti 4 055 503 011 17

TENAX

tenax.org

Warehouse-style Tenax is a Florentine clubbers' institution, offering a continually evolving mix of live bands and house sounds from the resident DJ and internationally known mixers. The Nobody's Perfect Party on Saturdays is *the* night out in the city.
Off map Via Pratese 46 055 308 160 Fri–Sat until 4am. Closed mid-May to Sep 29, 30

Where to Eat

PRICES

Prices are approximate, based on a 3-course meal without drinks for one person.

€€€ over €55
€€ €35–€55
€ under €35

Fiesole

LE CAVE DI MAIANO (€€–€€€)

Located just below Fiesole, the lovely patio terrace of this restaurant looks down over Florence, a perfect place for a summer dinner. Tuck into pasta with porcini mushrooms or wild boar sauce and perfectly grilled *bistecca* accompanied by a good Chianti.

Off map Via delle Cave di Maiano 16 055 591 33 Daily 12.30–3, 7.30–10.30 7

IL FIESOLANO (PERSEUS) (€€)

casatrattoria.com

This is one of Fiesole's best restaurants in which to sample the famous *bistecca alla fiorentina* (T-bone steak, ▷ panel). Other classic Tuscan dishes are served on a terrace at the back, facing the Teatro Romano in Fiesole.

Off map Piazza Mino da Fiesole 9 055 591 43 Mon–Sat 12.30–2.30, 7.30–10.30 7

LA LOGGIA, VILLA SAN MICHELE (€€€)

belmond.com

The evocative former monastery setting and some of the finest cuisine in the area attract diners to this elegant restaurant in the Villa San Michele. The views take in the whole city.

Off map Via Doccia 4 055 567 8200 Daily 1–2.30, 7.30–10.30; closed end Nov to end Mar 7

Lucca

BUCA DI SANT ANTONIO (€€)

bucadisantantonio.com

The menu here, one of the oldest as well as the most popular restaurants in Lucca, is all à la carte, with an emphasis on Lucchese cuisine, and the use of seasonal, freshly produced ingredients.

Via della Cervia 3 0583 558 81 Tue–Sat 12–2.30, 7.30–10, Sun 12–2.30

DA LEO (€)

trattoriadaleo.it

Da Leo is a popular, family-run trattoria where you can eat in the dining room, with its pastel walls and wooden furnishings, or on the simple but shaded terrace. The owners make you feel at home, sometimes sitting and chatting after the meal.

Via Tegrimi 1 0583 492 236 Daily 12–3, 7.30–10.30

MACHIAVELLI (€–€€)

This small, central trattoria, a few paces from Piazza San Salvatore, serves predominantly Tuscan and Lucchese cuisine with the usual mixture of cold cuts, a range of interesting sausages, grilled meats, roasts and home-made pastas.

NATURALLY ROBUST

The classic Florentine dish is *bistecca alla fiorentina* (T-bone steak sold by the weight, usually 100g). Grilled and served rare with lemon wedges, it can be found on the menu in many Florentine restaurants. Other traditional dishes include *trippa alla fiorentina* (tripe stewed with tomatoes and served with Parmesan), *crostini* (toasted bread with a variety of toppings) and *panzanella* (a salad of crumbled bread tossed with tomatoes with olive oil, onions, basil and parsley).

The small but well-chosen wine list complements the cooking.
✉ Via C Battisti 28 ☎ 0583 467 219
🕐 Mon–Sat lunch and dinner

Pisa

LA BUCA (€–€€)

labuca.org

Located in the heart of Pisa, La Buca draws the crowds with its pleasant terrace and set-price menu, which offers Tuscan cuisine at a reasonable price. Dinner is a little more formal but still with lots of pizza and pasta choices.
✉ Via G Tassi 6/B ☎ 050 560 660
🕐 Sat–Thu 12.15–2.30, 7.15–10.30

DA BRUNO (€€–€€€)

anticatrattoriadabruno.it

This long-established trattoria serves traditional local cuisine. The two dining rooms have wood-beamed ceilings, long, elegant tables, and whitewashed walls covered with photographs of the famous people who have dined here. Reserve in advance.
✉ Via Luigi Bianchi 12 ☎ 050 560 818
🕐 Thu–Mon 12–3, 7–10.30, Wed 7–10.30

Siena

LE LOGGE (€€–€€€)

giannibrunelli.it

Located in a former medieval pharmacy, this charming restaurant, with its old wood and glass cabinets, is just off the Campo. The menu is full of classic Tuscan dishes. Reserve ahead.
✉ Via del Porrione 33 ☎ 0577 480 13
🕐 Mon–Sat 12–2.45, 7–10.45

SOTTO LE FONTI (€€)

sottolefonti.it

This renovated medieval building houses a charmingly old-fashioned restaurant. The menu is based on Sienese dishes, such as salami, game, or lamb chops with juniper. The scrumptious cakes and desserts are all home-made.
✉ Via Esterna Fontebranda 118 ☎ 0577 226 446 🕐 Daily 12.30–2.30, 7.30–10

ICE CREAM

Italian ice cream—*gelato*—is generally of very high quality. Italians would rather pay more and eat something made with fresh ingredients. So a basic ice cream is usually made with milk, cream, eggs and sugar, and the tastes are strikingly pure and direct. A popular choice is *crema*—egg custard—good with a scoop of intense dark chocolate or pungent coffee. People usually opt for a selection of *creme* or *frutte* (creams or fruit) and don't mix the two types. The best *gelaterie* serve fruit varieties made from whatever is in season.

LA TAVERNA DI SAN GIUSEPPE (€–€€)

tavernasangiuseppe.it

With its intimate, cellar-like dining room, this lively trattoria specializes in Tuscan food, with an emphasis on meat, although vegetarians are well catered to with a rich vegetable soup, *ribollita,* made with bread.
✉ Via Giovanni Duprè 132 ☎ 0577 422 86 🕐 Mon–Sat 12–2.30, 7–10; closed last 2 weeks in Jan and Jul

TRE CRISTI (€€–€€€)

trecristi.com

If you want to eat fish and seafood in Siena, this is the place, although they do meat very well too, and there is an extensive wine list. Housed in a 15th-century palazzo, the atmosphere is sober and elegant.
✉ Vicolo di Provenzano 1/7 ☎ 0577 280 608 🕐 Mon–Sat 12.30–2.30, 7.30–10

Florence is one of Italy's top destinations and hotels are, on the whole, expensive. Check the internet before leaving home to catch some seasonal deals. Staying out of season is your best bet.

Introduction

Choose from world-class hotels in historic buildings, ultrachic boutique hotels, family-run *pensiones* that haven't changed in decades—or rent a room in a private house.

Hotels

Tuscan hotels (*alberghi*) are graded by the regional authorities on a star rating of one to five. These refer to the facilities provided rather than character or comfort. Expect five- and four-star hotels to be grand, with superb facilities and service. Three-star hotels are more idiosyncratic. Prices can vary enormously, as can the public areas and staffing levels; but all rooms will have a TV, phone and private bathroom. One and two stars are relatively inexpensive, clean and comfortable, and rooms almost always have private bathrooms in two-star places. Air conditioning is normally provided from two stars and up. Breakfast is usually included but can be very basic.

Rooms to Rent

Signs saying rooms (*camere* or *zimmer*) are rooms to rent in private houses and are a good option if money is tight or you can't find a hotel. Local tourist offices keep a list.

Where to Stay

Florence is so compact that if you stay in the historic centre all the main sights will be on your doorstep. Staying farther out will usually be less expensive and you may still be able to walk into town—from Piazzale Michelangelo, for example, it's only 20 minutes to the Duomo.

RESERVATIONS

Florence is so popular that you will need to book in advance at whatever time of year you decide to visit. If you're booking in advance from home, make certain you get written confirmation and take it with you. Without this, you may turn up and find all knowledge of your booking denied. If you make an internet booking, print out your booking confirmation and take it with you.

From top: the Westin Excelsior; the Scoti; bags waiting to be picked up; Loggiato dei Serviti

Budget Hotels

PRICES

Expect to pay up to €130 per night in high season for a double room in a budget hotel

CAMPING

Campeggio Michelangelo, on the hills south of the Arno, is just a short bus ride from central Florence. It has hot showers, toilets, washing machines, electricity points, internet access, a supermarket and a bar that looks out over the city. There are 240 pitches. Open all year.

H8 Viale Michelangelo 80 055 681 1977; ecvacanze.it 12, 13

CASA PUCCI

casapucci.it

Steps from the lovely Piazza Santo Spirito and its lively nightlife, Signora Pucci's home occupies an ex-convent and offers five homey bedrooms, one with a four-poster. There's a kitchen that guests can use and a large courtyard garden for summer breakfasts.

D6 Via Santa Monaca 8 055 216 560 C3, D

CASA SCHLATTER

casaschlatter.florence.com

Although this ex-artists' residence is a little way from the city centre, bus links are good. The three guest rooms are individually furnished with antiques, and there is a pretty garden. The breakfast is delicious.

J3 Viale dei Mille 14 347 118 0215 10, 17

CESTELLI

hotelcestelli.com

Owned by a Florentine-Japanese couple, the Cestelli is a friendly gem close to the chic shops of Via de' Tornabuoni. The rooms are simply furnished but pristine, with old parquet floors and some antiques. Not all have bathrooms and no breakfast is provided.

E6 Borgo SS Apostoli 25 055 214 213 C3, D

JOHANNA I

antichedimorefiorentine.it

Occupying the first floor of a gracious 19th-century building near San Lorenzo and beautifully renovated, the 10 rooms are small but nicely furnished and there is a communal room with a fridge.

G3 Via Bonifacio Lupi 14 055 481 896 C2

SCOTI

hotelscoti.com

The Scoti is housed in an atmospheric 15th-century building in an excellent location directly opposite the Palazzo Strozzi, in the shopping haven of Via de' Tornabuoni. In addition, it offers great value and tons of period character. The 11 bedrooms are simple and light, and the lounge area has attractive 18th-century frescoes depicting Italian landscapes.

E6 Via de' Tornabuoni 7 055 292 128 C3

VILLA BETANIA

villabetania.it

Immersed in a beautiful garden, this ochre-coloured villa offers excellent value, fresh air and breakfast on the terrace in summer. Each of the 20 rooms is furnished in its own individual style but all are very clean, and the staff are friendly. A 10-minute walk downhill (or a bus ride) brings you to Porta Romana.

D9 Viale del Poggio Imperiale 23 055 222 243 38

Mid-Range Hotels

PRICES

Expect to pay between €130 and €300 per night in high season for a double room in a mid-range hotel

ANNALENA

annalena.com

In a Medici palazzo opposite the Boboli Gardens, this hotel was once the haunt of artists and writers. Some of the 20 rooms have terraces and views of the private Annalena gardens. It's a lovely, peaceful spot.

D8 Via Romana 34 055 222 402
36, 37, D

ANTICA DIMORE JOHLEA

antichedimorefiorentine.it

One of the assets of this six-room B&B is its panoramic roof terrace. The rooms are all beautifully done out with antiques and vibrant fabrics, and most have four-poster beds. There's a sitting room with an honesty bar.

G3 Via San Gallo 80 055 463 3292
C1, 1, 6, 11

CASCI

hotelcasci.com

Now a family-run hotel, with 24 immaculate, functional rooms, this old palazzo close to the Duomo was once home to the Italian composer Gioacchino Rossini. Although modernized, it still has some of its original 14th-century features.

F4 Via Cavour 13 055 211 686
C1

WHICH ROOM?

The room with a view is a much sought-after thing. However, it can often come with street noise. Most Florentine hotels are in palazzi built around courtyards, so the rooms with views face onto the street, while the ones looking over the courtyards are pleasantly quiet. You might prefer to forgo the romance to ensure a good night's sleep.

DAVANZATI

hoteldavanzati.it

You can't beat the location of this small hotel near Piazza della Signoria. Rooms are simply furnished but spotless; bathrooms are modern. Complimentary extras include iPads, hot drinks and cakes at teatime, and Happy Hour.

F6 Via Porta Rossa 5 055 286 666
C3, D

HERMITAGE

hermitagehotel.com

This well-known, 28-room hotel overlooks the Ponte Vecchio. Its light and airy roof garden is an idyllic place to relax after a day exploring the city.

F6 Vicolo Marzio 1, Piazza del Pesce
055 287 216 C3, D

LOGGIATO DEI SERVITI

loggiatodeiservitihotel.it

You can relax under vaulted ceilings, amid dark-wood antiques and rich fabrics in the former monastery of the Serviti. The 37 rooms are enlivened by bright curtains and throws. Many look onto the arcades of Piazza Santissima Annunziata and the breakfast room has views of the Accademia gardens.

G4 Piazza Santissima Annunziata 3
055 289 592 C1, C2, 6

MARIO'S

hotelmarios.com

This family-run hotel exemplifies the great value for money that can still be found in this expensive city. It feels as if you are staying in someone's home,

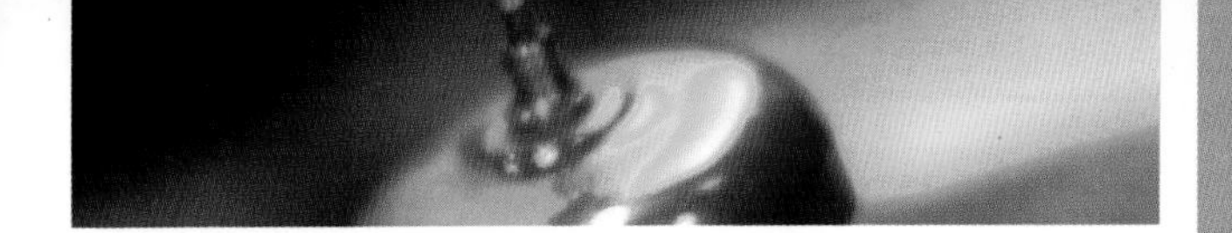

with care and attention paid to the 16 atmospheric rooms and to your needs.
E4 Via Faenza 89 055 216 801
T1

PALAZZO GALLETTI

palazzogalletti.it

This 11-room hotel occupies the first floor of a 16th-century palazzo. The smart bedrooms are a mix of old and new; most have small balconies over-looking the internal courtyard. The two suites are huge and feature original floor-to-ceiling frescoes.

G5 Via Sant'Egidio 12 055 390 5750 C1, C2

PALAZZO GUADAGNI

palazzoguadagni.com

Set on a lively square in the Oltrarno, this lovely hotel features huge fireplaces, frescoed ceilings and oak beams. Factor in modern amenities, antique furniture and some of the loveliest views in the city—especially from the loggia—and you have a great place to stay.

E7 Piazza Santo Spirito 9 055 265 8376 C3, D

RELAIS GRAND TOUR

florencegrandtour.com

Standing on a quiet residential street, this delightful hotel offers just four rooms, all thoughtfully furnished with antiques. There's a pretty courtyard, and owners Giuseppe and Cristina are full of helpful advice. Breakfast coupons are available at the local bar.

F4 Via Santa Reparata 21 055 283 955 C1, 6, 11

LA SCALETTA

hotellascaletta.com

For those who want to stay on the quieter south side of the River Arno, La Scaletta is a good choice. The hotel is just steps away from the Ponte Vecchio, the Pitti Palace and the Boboli Gardens. The 30 rooms have a homey feel and there is a lovely rooftop terrace.

E7 Via de Guicciardini 13 055 283 028 D

SOPRARNO SUITES

soprarnosuites.com

Inhabiting two floors of a Renaissance palazzo in the Oltrarno, this gorgeous hotel has 11 highly individual rooms featuring lofty, frescoed ceilings, an intriguing collection of retro furnishings, in-room bathtubs and fabulous bath-rooms. Breakfast—with home-made cakes—is delicious.

E7 Via Maggio 35 055 046 8718
C3, D

TORNABUONI BEACCI

tornabuonihotels.com

Well-placed for shopping and sight-seeing, this handsome hotel has a large, leafy roof garden and antiques-filled lounge, which are quiet retreats from the bustle of the city outside on this busy street. The 60 bedrooms are simple and uncluttered, decorated with antique furnishings.

E6 Via de' Tornabuoni 3 055 212 645 C2, C3

VILLA FIESOLE

villafiesole.it

In the hilltop village of Fiesole, this hotel with 32 rooms has an outdoor pool and a wonderful Victorian green-house that accommodates the breakfast room, a lounge area and several bed-rooms. This hotel offers really good value for great surroundings.

Off map at M1 Via Beato Angelico 35
055 597 252 7

Luxury Hotels

Expect to pay over €300 per night in high season for a double room in a luxury hotel

FOUR SEASONS FLORENCE

fourseasons.com/florence

It may be a little way from the city centre, but the service and facilities at this luxury resort more than compensate. Apart from the magnificent public rooms and bedrooms, there is a huge garden, a fabulous spa and gym and a Michelin-starred restaurant.

H4 Borgo Pinti 99 055 262 61 6, 8, 14

HELVETIA & BRISTOL

hotelhelvetiabristol.com

With its old-world atmosphere and superb location near the Duomo, this grand, 18th-century hotel is a great choice. All the rooms are decorated with opulent fabrics and antique furnishings. Breakfast is served in a belle époque winter garden, while Hostaria Bibendum (▷ 49) offers fine dining in the evening.

E5 Via dei Pescioni 2 055 266 51 C2

J. K. PLACE

jkplace.com

This small, chic hotel is a fabulous blend of old and new, where modern art is cleverly displayed alongside antique features. The sleek bedrooms and homey day rooms are decorated with great attention to detail. There's a pleasant rooftop terrace on Piazza Santa Maria Novella.

E5 Piazza Santa Maria Novella 7 055 264 5181 All buses to Santa Maria Novella station

PORTRAIT FIRENZE

lungarnocollection.com

For the ultimate in luxury and a magnificent riverside location, book into Ferragamo-owned Portrait Firenze. The soft grey rooms all have mini kitchens and the latest in high-tech gadgetry.

F6 Lungarno degli Acciaiuoli 4 055 2726 4000 C3, D

ST. REGIS FLORENCE

stregisflorence.com

Florence's opulent St. Regis occupies a 19th-century palazzo on the north bank of the Arno with 107 gorgeously decorated rooms, the best of which have a river view. The myriad facilities include a spa and a Michelin-starred restaurant, the Winter Garden.

D5 Piazza Ognissanti 1 055 271 61 A, B

SAVOY

roccofortehotels.com

The Savoy enjoys a fabulous location right on Piazza della Repubblica and steps from the Duomo. It offers stylish, understated luxury in its 88 rooms and 14 suites, plus a cocktail bar and restaurant with a terrace right on the buzzing square.

F5 Piazza della Republicca 7 055 27351 C2

WESTIN EXCELSIOR

westinflorence.com

A hotel in the grand style, the 171-room Westin Excelsior is located right on the Arno; try to book one of the many rooms with watery views. Top-floor gourmet restaurant SE.STO (▷ 50) has views of the whole city; book in for a sunset cocktail at the very least.

D5 Piazza Ognissanti 3 055 271 51 C3, D

Florence is compact and the public transportation good. Walking is probably one of the best and most rewarding ways of getting around. Petty crime is common but the city is relatively safe.

Planning Ahead

When to Go

Florence's peak season runs from March to October, although many consider it virtually uninterrupted. The city is overrun with tour groups in May, June and July. If you like heat, go in August—although many Florentines are on holiday and some restaurants close, it's a good time to go because everything is quieter.

TIME

Italy is one hour ahead of London, six hours ahead of New York and nine hours ahead of Los Angeles.

AVERAGE DAILY MAXIMUM TEMPERATURES

JAN	FEB	MAR	APR	MAY	JUN	JUL	AUG	SEP	OCT	NOV	DEC
50°F	52°F	59°F	64°F	73°F	79°F	84°F	82°F	79°F	70°F	57°F	54°F
10°C	11°C	15°C	18°C	23°C	26°C	29°C	28°C	26°C	21°C	14°C	12°C

Spring (March to May) is a good time to visit if you want to avoid the summer heat.
Summer (June to August) can be extremely hot and humid, often uncomfortably so in July and August.
Autumn (September to November) is generally the wettest time in Tuscany, and thunderstorms are common in September.
Winter (December to February) temperatures are often chilly, and rainfall can be high. However, the city is at its emptiest at this time (if you avoid Christmas and New Year).

WHAT'S ON

January *Pitti Immagine:* Fashion shows at the Fortezza da Basso.
February *Carnevale:* A low-key version of Venice's annual extravaganza.
March *Festa dell'Annunziata* (25 Mar): Traditionally the Florentine new year, with a fair to celebrate in Piazza Santissima Annunziata.
Scoppio del Carro: The Easter Sunday service at the Duomo culminates in an exploding carriage full of fireworks.
April *Mostra Mercato Internazionale dell' Artigianato:* An international arts and crafts festival in the Fortezza da Basso.
May/June *Maggio Musicale:* Florence's international music and dance festival.
Festa del Grillo (Sun after Ascension): Crickets are sold in cages, then released in the park of Le Cascine (▷ 98).
June *Calcio in Costume:* An elaborate soccer game between town districts, played in medieval costume in Piazza Santa Croce; preceded by a procession.
Festa di San Giovanni (24 Jun): Fireworks in Piazzale Michelangelo (▷ 87) celebrate the feast of Florence's patron saint.
Estate Fiesolana (mid-Jun to Sep): A Fiesole arts festival.
September *Festa del Rificolona* (7 Sep): Children carry paper lanterns in Piazza Santissima Annunziata to honour the birth of the Virgin.
October *Amici della Musica* (Oct–Apr): Concerts. Tickets from Teatro della Pergola (☎ 055 226 4316).
November *Festival dei Popoli* (Nov–Dec): A film festival in the Odeon Cinehall (▷ 46), showing international films.

Florence Online

enit.it
Florence is particularly well covered on the Italian Tourist Board website, with information on history, culture, events, accommodation and gastronomy, in several languages.

turismo.intoscana.it
Run by the Tuscan Regional Tourist Board, this site covers the whole region, including Florence.

comune.fi.it
Florence City Council site has good information in English. Its tourism, museum and art pages are always up-to-date, with some good links.

firenzeturismo.it
The official APT tourism site with plenty of useful information in English.

firenze.net
This Florence-based site, in Italian and English, has information on where to go and what to do, with good maps and plenty of links.

emmeti.it
Another Italy-based site, in Italian and English, with a good range of information and links for Florence. It is strong on local events and has an online hotel reservation service.

initaly.com
This lively US site is clearly run by passionate Italophiles and has excellent planning tips and sightseeing hints.

florence.hotelguide.net
florence.hotelsfinder.com
Useful online hotel booking sites for Florence and other Italian destinations.

firenzemusei.it
You can reserve a timed entrance ticket, to avoid a long wait, to the main Florentine museums, including the Uffizi, via this efficient site.

USEFUL SITES

fodors.com
A complete travel-planning site. You can research prices and weather; book air tickets, cars and rooms; ask questions (and get answers) from fellow travellers; and find links to other sites.

trenitalia.com
The official site of the Italian State Railways.

weatheronline.co.uk/Italy.htm
Good three-day weather predictions.

INTERNET ACCESS

Florence is rapidly coming into the 21st-century with its online facilities. WiFi hotspots can be found all over the city, including Piazza Duomo, Piazza della Repubblica, Piazza della Signoria, Piazza Santo Spirito and Santa Maria Novella station. Many bars, cafés and restaurants offer free internet access, as do most hotels.

Getting There

DIRECT FLIGHTS

There are no direct intercontinental flights to Florence so visitors have to fly to Milan (298km/185 miles north), Rome (277km/172 miles south) or another European city, then take a connecting flight or train. The flight from New York to Rome takes around nine hours; from the airport, take a shuttle train to Stazione Termini, then a train to Florence (1.5 hours).

ENTRY REQUIREMENTS

Check the latest passport and visa information before you travel; look up the British embassy website at gov.uk/government/world/italy or the United States embassy at usembassy.gov. EU citizens do not require visas to visit Italy.

CUSTOMS REGULATIONS

- EU nationals do not have to declare goods imported for their personal use.
- The limits for non-EU visitors are 200 cigarettes or 100 small cigars or 250g of tobacco; 1 litre of alcohol (over 22 per cent alcohol) or 2 litres of fortified wine; 60ml of perfume.

AIRPORTS

You can choose from three airports—Galileo Galilei Airport at Pisa, the small Amerigo Vespucci Airport at Florence and Guglielmo Marconi Airport at Bologna. The flight takes approximately 2 hours from London.

FROM FLORENCE AIRPORT

Amerigo Vespucci Airport (tel 055 306 1300, aeroporto.firenze.it), also known as Peretola, is 4km (2.5 miles) northwest of the city. It handles domestic and European flights. The airport is connected to the city centre by the light blue Volainbus shuttle (administered by ATAF and SITA, tel 800 424 500, ataf.net), which runs every 30 minutes from 6am to 8.30pm, then every hour until 11.30pm, to Santa Maria Novella station. The journey takes 20 minutes and tickets, which cost €6, can be bought on board. Taxis cost around €22, plus possible surcharges (agree a price before you set off).

FROM PISA AIRPORT

Pisa's Galileo Galilei Airport (tel 050 849 300, pisa-airport.com), the region's main point of entry, lies 80km (50 miles) west of Florence. The one spacious terminal handles domestic and European flights. A new driverless train service, the People Mover, connecting Pisa airport and Pisa Centrale train station every 5–8 minutes, is due to be inaugurated in 2017. This will run between 6am and midnight daily. Until then, a bus makes the same journey every 10

minutes, stopping just outside the airport terminal. Tickets are available in the arrivals hall. A single ticket to Florence costs €9.70, including the bus. Terravision (terravision.eu) runs an unreliable airport bus transfer, taking around 70 minutes, to Florence train station between 8.40am and 12.20am, costing €5 one way, €10 round-trip. A taxi to Florence could cost you more than €130. There is a helpful information office inside the terminal where you can buy tickets for trains and the bus.

FROM BOLOGNA AIRPORT

Guglielmo Marconi Airport (tel 051 647 9615, bologna-airport.it) is 105km (65 miles) northeast of Florence in the Emilia-Romagna region and handles a large volume of European charter and scheduled flights, as well as budget airline flights. A shuttle bus costing about €6 takes passengers to Bologna Centrale station (grandistazioni.it). From here the journey takes about 35 minutes and costs around €26, depending on the type of train taken. Make sure your ticket is valid for the right train. Rental cars are available in Terminal A. Taxis to Florence cost about €220.

ARRIVING BY TRAIN

The main station, Santa Maria Novella (grandistazioni.it), has links with major Italian cities. Most buses in Florence depart from the station forecourt, and there are usually taxis waiting. Don't forget to validate your ticket, by inserting it into the yellow box on the platform, before boarding your train. Fast services that don't terminate in Florence may stop at Campo di Marte station instead, which is just outside the ring road, near the football stadium; catch another train to Santa Maria Novella from here.

ARRIVING BY LONG-DISTANCE BUS

Lazzi runs express services to and from Rome and links Florence with major European cities as part of the Eurolines network (Via Mercadante 2, tel 055 363 041, lazzi.it).

TRAVEL INSURANCE

Take out your insurance as soon as you book your trip to ensure you are covered for delays. Most policies cover cancellation, medical expenses, accident compensation, personal liability and loss of personal belongings (including money). Your policy should cover the cost of getting you home in case of medical emergency. An annual travel policy may be the best value if you intend to make several trips in a year away from home, but long trips abroad may not be covered. If you have private medical coverage, check your policy, as you may be covered while you are away.

CAR RENTAL

The major car rental groups are all represented in the region and have offices at airports, rail stations and in the bigger cities.

Getting Around

STREET NUMBERS

One building can have two totally different numbers in Florence. The red system is for shops, restaurants and businesses; the blue system is for hotels or residences.

VISITORS WITH DISABILITIES

As in many other historic Italian cities, visitors with disabilities are far from well served in Florence, though things are improving. The official APT website (▷ 115) has detailed information for tourists with special needs. Many city museums are fully wheelchair-accessible, with ramps, elevators and suitable bathrooms. The grey and green buses can take wheelchairs, as does the electric D bus, which goes through the heart of Florence (board via the electric platform at the rear door). Taxis do take wheelchairs but it is wise to let them know when you make a reservation.

The Tuscan capital has no metro or subway system, but the *centro storico* (historic centre) is largely traffic-free and can be crossed on foot in 30 minutes. There is an efficient bus service linking the outskirts of the city to the central areas, and a fleet of small electric buses serves the *centro storico*. The city is in the middle of major work to install a tram system. The first phase, linking Santa Maria Novella station with the western suburb of Scandicci, is complete; two more routes are under construction. Azienda Trasporti Area Fiorentina (ATAF) is responsible for public transportation (ataf.net).

BUSES

Bus routes in Florence are numbered and many start and end at the railway station at regular intervals. The zippy little electric buses that run through the *centro storico*, identified by letters (C1, C2, C3 and D), link all kinds of places in the narrow streets of the old city. Buy tickets at bars, tobacconists and from the ATAF booth on Piazza Stazione before boarding. Once on board, insert your ticket into the small orange box and it will be stamped with the time. Failure to validate your ticket can result in a hefty fine. The ticket is valid for the next 90 minutes for any bus; it costs €1.20 or €2 if purchased on board. A multiple ticket gives you four 90-minute tickets and costs €4.70. The tourist information office by the station has bus maps.

HOP-ON-HOP-OFF BUS

If you really want to avoid any leg work, or want an overview of how the city is laid out, take an open-top bus ride with City Sightseeing (tel 055 290 451, city-sightseeing.it). This bus permits visitors to get on and off at any number of designated stops on the tourist itinerary. The ticket is valid for 24 hours and costs €23.

LONG-DISTANCE BUS

There are three main bus companies in Florence:

- Lazzi at Via Mercadante 2, tel 055 363 041, lazzi.it.

• SITA serves southern and eastern Tuscany (Via Santa Caterina da Siena 17, tel 055 219 383 in Italy only, sitabus.it).
• CAP serves the region to the northeast of Florence, the Mugello (Largo Fratelli Alinari 9, tel 055 214 637, capautolinee.it).

TAXIS
The official white Florentine taxis are clean and comfortable. You cannot hail them on the street; instead you must pick them up at a taxi rank at key locations such as the station, Piazza del Duomo, Piazza della Repubblica, or call one of the official cab companies: Radio Taxi SO.CO. TA. (tel 055 410 133) or Radio Taxi 4390 (tel 055 4390). The meter starts running the moment your call is received. Supplements are charged for baggage and at night.

BICYCLES AND MOTORCYCLES
Bicycles can be rented from Florence by Bike at Via San Zanobi 54r (tel 055 488 992, florencebybike.it).

Mopeds and motorcycles can be rented from Alinari at Via Zanobi 38r (tel 055 280 500, alinarirental.com).

CARS
It is really not worth driving around Florence. Much of the city is closed to traffic, there is a one-way system and parking is difficult. However, a car is ideal if you plan to tour the Tuscan countryside. If you do rent a car, try to book a hotel with parking.
Main car rental companies are:
• Avis, Borgo Ognissanti 128r, tel 055 213 629.
• Europcar, Borgo Ognissanti 53–55r, tel 055 290 438.
• Hertz Italiana, Borgo Ognissanti 137, tel 055 239 8205.

Driving around outside the city is easy. Tolls are payable on highways (*autostrade*). Most, but by no means all, fuel stations take credit cards. You can contact Highway emergency/ Breakdown service (ACI) on 803 116.

TIPS

• You should board a bus through the front or rear door, but exit through the middle ones.
• Children travel free if they are less than 1m (3ft 3in) in height. Their height is checked against the box that you validate your ticket in.
• Smoking is not allowed on buses.
• Most buses are adapted for people with disabilities.
• Bus routes are not always the same on the return leg so check the map at the bus stop to be sure you can get off at the stop of your choice.

OTHER TRANSPORTATION

• A novel way of getting around is to rent a Segway, a two-wheeled self-balancing electric vehicle (☎ 055 239 8885; segwayfirenze.com).
• Hail a pedicab or bicycle rickshaw—with room enough for two adults or one adult and two children (pedicabfirenze.it).
• Horse-drawn carriages known as *fiacchere* offer hour-long city tours and depart from various venues (see tourist office). These have the bonus of being able to enter small pedestrian streets.

Essential Facts

PRESS

- The Florentines' preferred newspaper is *La Nazione*, a national paper produced in Florence.
- You can buy foreign newspapers and magazines at the station and at Sorbi, the kiosk in Piazza della Signoria.

MONEY

The euro is the official currency of Italy. Bank notes come in denominations of 5, 10, 20, 50, 100, 200 and 500 euros, and coins in denominations of 1, 2, 5, 10, 20 and 50 cents and 1 and 2 euros.

ELECTRICITY

- Voltage is 220 volts and sockets take two round pins.

EMERGENCY TELEPHONE NUMBERS

- Police: 113; 112 (Carabinieri)
- Fire: 115
- Ambulance: 118
- State Police headquarters is on Via Zara 2 (tel 055 497 71).

ETIQUETTE

- Make the effort to speak some Italian; it will be appreciated.
- Shake hands on introduction and leaving; once you know people better you can replace this with a kiss on each cheek.
- Use the polite form for "you", *lei*, unless the other person uses *tu*.
- Always say *buon giorno* (hello) and *arrivederci* (goodbye) in shops.
- Italians do not get drunk in public.
- Smoking is banned in enclosed public spaces.

LOST PROPERTY

- Lost property office: Via Veracini 5 (tel 055 334 802, open Mon–Wed, Fri–Sat 9–12).
- Report losses of passports to the police and other items to the Questura at Via Zara 2 (tel 055 49771).
- There's also a lost property office at Stazione Santa Maria Novella (tel 055 235 6120, open daily 4.15pm–1.30am).

MAIL

- Main post office: Via Pellicceria 3 (tel 055 273 6481, poste.it, open Mon–Sat 8.15–7).
- There is another big post office at Via Pietrapiana 53–55 (tel 055 267 4231, open Mon–Fri 8.15–7, Sat 8.15–12.30).
- Stamps (*francobolli*) can be purchased from post offices or from tobacconists displaying a white T sign on a black or blue background.
- Post boxes are small, red and marked "Poste" or "Lettere." The slot on the left is for addresses

within the city and the slot on the right is for other destinations.

MEDICINES AND MEDICAL TREATMENT

- EU nationals receive reduced-cost medical treatment on production of the relevant document (EHIC card for Britons, at least until Brexit is finalized). Private medical insurance for UK and all other nationals is still advised.
- For medical emergencies, call 118.
- Medical Service Firenze (Via Roma 4, tel 055 475 411) has English-speaking doctors. Phone for an appointment or call out, or just drop in to the walk-in clinic (Mon–Fri 11–12, 1–3, 5–6, Sat 11–12, 1–3).
- Hospital: Santa Maria Nuova is at Piazza Santa Maria Nuova 1, call 055 69381.
- Interpreters can be arranged for free through Ospedale di Careggi (surgical accident and emergency unit) at Viale Pieraccini 17 (tel 055 794 111/ 7057, Mon–Sat 8.30–12.30). They can also advise if you need dental services.
- Pharmacies are indicated by a large green or red cross. For pharmacy information, call 800 420 707 (toll-free from within Italy).
- All-night pharmacies:

Comunale 13 della Stazione, at the train station (tel 055 216 761)
All'Insegna del Moro-Taverna, Piazza San Giovanni 20r (tel 055 211 343)
Molteni, at Via dei Calzaiuoli 7r (tel 055 289 490)

MONEY AND CREDIT CARDS

- Credit cards are widely accepted.
- ATMs are now plentiful.

NATIONAL HOLIDAYS

- 1 Jan: New Year's Day; 6 Jan: Epiphany; Easter Sunday; Easter Monday; 25 Apr: Liberation Day; 1 May: Labour Day; 2 Jun: Repubblica Day; 24 June: Feast of San Giovanni (Florence only);15 Aug: Assumption; 1 Nov: All Saints' Day; 8 Dec: Immaculate Conception; 25 Dec: Christmas Day; 26 Dec: St. Stephen's Day.

TOILETS

- Italian toilets are generally improving both in cleanliness and facilities.
- Expect to pay about €1 for toilets. Those away from the main tourist areas are usually free.
- There are 22 public toilets in Piazza San Giovanni, near the Baptistery.
- Most bars and cafés have toilets and usually allow anybody to use them (although it's polite to have at least a drink).
- Florence has promoted the initiative "Courtesy Point" in which several bars and cafés have made their toilets available to the public.

CONSULATES

British Consulate
✉ Lungarno Corsini 2
☎ 055 284 133
Spanish Honorary Consul
✉ Via dei Servi 13 ☎ 055 212 207
US Consulate ✉ Lungarno Amerigo Vespucci 38
☎ 055 266 951

PRECAUTIONS

- Take care of wallets, handbags and backpacks as pickpockets target tourists.
- Keep the receipts and numbers of your traveller's cheques separately from the traveller's cheques.
- Keep a copy of the front page of your passport.
- List the numbers and expiration dates of your credit cards and keep the list separately.
- If a theft occurs, make a statement (*denuncia*) at a police station within 24 hours if you wish to make an insurance claim.
- After dark avoid Le Cascine and the station.

OPENING TIMES

- Banks: generally Mon–Fri 8.30–1.30, 2.30–4. Some banks also open Saturday mornings.
- Post offices: Mon–Fri 8.15–1.30, Sat 8.15–12.30.
- Shops: normally Mon–Sat 8.30–1 and from 3 or 4 until 7 or 8; larger stores in city centre 10–7.
- Museums: see individual entries.
- Churches: 7 or 8–12.30 and then from 3 or 4 until 7.30. Main tourist attractions often stay open longer. No two are the same.

TELEPHONES

- Public phones are silver and orange, but these are few and far between.
- Few public telephones take coins. Phone cards (*carta* or *scheda* or *tessera telefonica*) are the most practical way to use a public phone.
- Directory Inquiries: call 1254.
- International directory inquiries: call 1254.
- International operator: call 1254; you can also make reverse charge international calls on this number via the operator.
- Cheap rate is all day Sunday and 9pm–8am (national) on other days; 10pm–8am (international).
- To call Italy from the UK, dial 00 followed by 39 (the code for Italy) then the number. To call the UK from Italy dial 00 44 then drop the first zero from the area code.
- To call Italy from the US dial 011 followed by 39. To call the US from Italy dial 00 1.
- Florence's area code (055) must always be dialled even if you are calling from within Florence.

TOURIST INFORMATION OFFICE

- The principal tourist office can be found at Via Cavour 1r (tel 055 290 832/3, firenzeturismo.it, Mon–Sat 8.15–7.15, Sun 8.30–1.30).
- Tourists can also call the Tourist Contact Center (tel 055 000, daily 9am–7pm) for information, or email touristinfo@comune.fi.it.

Language

Italian pronunciation is totally consistent. Cs and gs are hard when they are followed by an a, o or u (as in "cat" and "got"), and soft if followed by an e or an i (as in "child" or "geranium"). The Tuscans often pronounce their cs and chs as hs.

USEFUL WORDS AND PHRASES	
buon giorno	good morning
buona sera	good afternoon/ evening
buona notte	good night
ciao	hello/ goodbye (informal)
arrivederci	goodbye (informal)
arrivederla	goodbye (formal)
per favore	please
grazie	thank you
prego	you're welcome
come sta/stai?	how are you?
sto bene	I'm fine
mi dispiace	I'm sorry
scusi/scusa	excuse me/ I beg your pardon
permesso	excuse me (in a crowd)
quant'è?	how much is it?
quando?	when?
avete...?	do you have...?
qui/qua	here

EMERGENCIES	
aiuto!	help!
dov'è il telefono più vicino?	where is the nearest telephone?
c'è stato un incidente	there has been an accident
chiamate la polizia	call the police
chiamate un medico/ un'ambulanza	call a doctor/ an ambulance
pronto soccorso	first aid
dov'è l'ospedale più vicino?	where is the nearest hospital?

BASIC VOCABULARY	
sì	yes
no	no
non ho capito	I don't under-stand
sinistra	left
destra	right
entrata	entrance
uscita	exit
aperto	open
chiuso	closed
buono	good
cattivo	bad
grande	big
piccolo	small
con	with
senza	without
più	more

NUMBERS	
uno/primo	1/first
due/ secondo	2/second
tre/terzo	3/third
quattro/ quarto	4/fourth
cinque/ quinto	5/fifth
sei	6
sette	7
otto	8
nove	9
dieci	10
venti	20
cinquanta	50
cento	100
mille	1,000
milione	1,000,000

Timeline

THE FLORIN

Florence minted its own coins, florins, in silver in 1235 and in gold in 1252. Soon they were being used as the standard coin in Europe, evidence of the pre-eminence of Florence in European finance.

BEFORE 1000

Florence started to grow in 59BC as a result of an agrarian law passed by Julius Caesar, granting land to retired army veterans. Byzantine walls were added to the Roman walls in AD541–44, as protection against the Ostrogoths. The Lombards took Tuscany in 570 but were defeated in the early ninth century by Charlemagne. Florence then became part of the Holy Roman Empire, ruled by imperial princes known as Margraves.

1115 The first comune (city state) is formed. Florence is run by a 100-strong assembly.

1250–60 The Primo Popolo regime controls Florence, dominated by trade guilds.

1296 The building of the Duomo begins, under Arnolfo di Cambio.

1340s Florence faces economic crisis after Edward III of England bankrupts the Peruzzi and Bardi and the Black Death plague halves the population.

1378 The uprising of the *ciompi* (wool carders) is the high point of worker unrest.

1406 Florence captures Pisa, gaining direct access to the sea.

1458 Cosimo de' Medici is recognized as ruler of Florence.

1469–92 Lorenzo the Magnificent rules.

1494 Florence surrenders to Charles VIII of France. Savonarola, a zealous monk, takes control of the city.

1498 Savonarola is burned at the stake after four years of rule, and Florence becomes a republic.

1502 The Republic of Florence retakes Pisa.

1570 Cosimo I creates a Tuscan state free from the Holy Roman Empire.

1743 Anna Maria Luisa, last of the Medici, dies. Florence is then ruled by the house of Lorraine under Francis Stephen.

1799–1814 Tuscany is occupied by Napoleon's troops.

1865–70 Florence becomes the capital of Italy. King Vittorio Emanuele is installed in the Pitti Palace.

1944 On 4 August, Germans blow up all the bridges in Florence with the exception of the Ponte Vecchio.

1966 The River Arno bursts its banks without warning on 4 November: Florence is flooded, the waters reaching to more than 6m (20ft) in some areas.

1993 The Uffizi Gallery is bombed by the Mafia and five people killed.

2004 Michelangelo's *David* is unveiled after controversial restoration.

2010 Annual visitor numbers to Florence (population 370,000) top the six million mark.

2016 Vasari's *Last Supper* (1543), restored after being badly damaged in the 1966 flood, is unveiled in the Museo dell'Opera di Santa Croce.

FAMOUS FLORENTINES

The poet Dante Alighieri, author of the *Divine Comedy*, was born in Florence in 1265. He was exiled from the city in 1302 because of his sympathies with the White Guelphs, and died in 1321.

Michelangelo Buonarroti (1475–1564) created some of his most famous works in Florence, including the sculpture *David*. Born in Caprese, he was buried in Florence's Santa Croce.

Political philosopher Niccolò Machiavelli was born in Florence in 1469.

Galileo Galilei (1564–1642), from Pisa, spent much of his life in Florence as the Medici court mathematician.

From far left: Bust of Cosimo di Giovanni de' Medici and on his horse; Napoleon Bonaparte; Dante Alighieri; fleur-de-lys guild emblem; the defensive Forte di Belvedere

Index

CityPack Florence

Published by AA Publishing, a trading name of AA Media Limited, whose registered office is Fanum House, Basing View, Basingstoke, Hampshire RG21 4EA. Registered number 06112600.

First published 1997
Revised and updated 2015
New edition 2018

Written by Susannah Perry
Additional writing Jackie Staddon and Hilary Weston
Updated by Sally Roy
Series editor Clare Ashton
Design work Liz Baldin
Image retouching and repro Ian Little

Colour separation by AA Digital Department
Printed and bound by Leo Paper Products, China

A CIP catalogue record for this book is available from the British Library.

ISBN 978-0-7495-7935-7

We have tried to ensure accuracy in this guide, but things do change, so plea
let us know if you have any comments at travelguides@theAA.com.

A05542
Maps in this title produced from mapping © MAIRDUMONT / Falk Verlag 2
Transport map © Communicarta Ltd, UK

Titles in the Series

- Amsterdam
- Bangkok
- Barcelona
- Berlin
- Boston
- Brussels & Bruges
- Budapest
- Dublin
- Edinburgh
- Florence
- Hong Kong
- Istanbul
- Las Vegas
- Lisbon
- London
- Madrid
- Milan
- Munich
- New York
- Orlando
- Paris
- Prague
- Rome
- San Francisco
- Singapore
- Sydney
- Toronto
- Venice
- Vienna
- Washington